JEAN JACQUES ROUSSEAU

his educational theories
selected from

ÉMILE

Julie and Other Writings

EDITED BY
R. L. ARCHER
PROFESSOR OF EDUCATION
UNIVERSITY OF COLLEGE OF NORTH WALES
Bangor, Wales

WITH A BIOGRAPHICAL NOTE BY
S. E. FROST JR.
Brooklyn College
Brooklyn, New York

Barron's Educational Series, inc.
WOODBURY, NEW YORK

JEAN JACQUES ROUSSEAU

BIOGRAPHICAL NOTE

Rousseau the Man

His life story. Born in Geneva of a French father and a Swiss mother who died when he was one week old, Rousseau was reared by his father, an eccentric and sentimental watchmaker. His father taught him to read but did not train him in the conventional habits and attitudes of normal life. Thus, he stole, lied, played dirty tricks, was indolent, ill-bred, and unprincipled. His father left Geneva when Rousseau was ten, and the boy went to Bossey to school. Returning to Geneva several years later, he failed as a clerk, was apprenticed to an engraver but ran away at sixteen and became a vagabond. He became a Catholic, met Madame de Warrens, attempted to find himself in the priesthood, in music, and in teaching, but failed in each case. His wanderings showed him the miseries of the peasants and his studies introduced him to the current thought regarding social and philosophical problems. In 1741 he went to Paris, entered the society of leaders of the Enlightenment, and lived with Thérèse Lavasseur, who bore him five children. His genius awakened with a flash in October, 1749. He wrote the prize essay, *Discourse on the Arts and Sciences.* This was followed by *What Is the Cause of Inequality Among Men?,*

JEAN JACQUES ROUSSEAU

The New Heloise, The Social Contract, Emile, Confessions.
His life was a psychological puzzle—highly emotional, erratic, a creative genius, a man of reprobate and perverted nature, an idealist, passionately devoted to the downtrodden and to liberty.

ROUSSEAU THE POLITICAL AND SOCIAL THEORIST

His revolt against civilization. The Academy of Dijon offered, in the *Mercure de France*, a prize for an answer to the question: "Has the restoration of the Arts and Sciences had a purifying effect upon morals?" Rousseau answered that in all ages the arts and sciences had caused the downfall of morals.

His theory of social development. 1. Natural Man: Original man in the state of nature is an animal. His aim is to avoid pain and death and to satisfy his physical wants for food, a mate, and rest. He is motivated by the impulse for self-preservation (*amour-de-soi* or self-love). All men are equal and free at this stage and no one is dependent upon another.

2. Savage Man: Reason makes man more than an animal and he develops speech, family life, and simple arts, but he is independent, has few wants, and his virtues are greater than his vices.

3. Civilized Man: Man's imagination brings new desires and he creates civilization. Primitive self-love gives way to a calculated and ambitious love of self (*amour-propre*). This creates all the evils of society and leads to man's degradation. Man's reason leads to inequality and destroys the primitive state of innocence. Thus, Rousseau prayed for deliverance from "the fatal arts and sciences of our forefathers" and a return to "ignorance, innocence, and poverty which alone can make us happy."

JEAN JACQUES ROUSSEAU

4. The Way to Happiness: To rescue man from this condition, Rousseau called for reforms in state, church, marriage, family life, and the schools. In the State: Liberty is a natural right. By a social contract man established the state. This state must protect man and preserve his original freedom. The state must be governed by a direct democracy and all laws should be a direct expression of the general will. This doctrine shows development between his writing of the *Discourse on the Arts and Sciences* and *The Social Contract*. In the Church: In his *Profession of Faith of a Savoyard Vicar* he pleads for a religion based on nature and reason. In Marriage and Family Life: In *The New Heloise* he condemns marriages arranged by parents without the consent of the children. He holds that marriage should be based upon natural feelings and affections.

His doctrine of evil. Rousseau opposed the doctrine of original sin and held that "everything is good as it comes from the hands of the author of nature." Vice begins when man enters into human relations. These relations create self-centered interests which conflict with those of other individuals. The home, school, and social environment give children artificial desires that result in conflicts and evils. To realize desires men use others and social inequality results, leading to degeneracy and evil in society and in the individual.

ROUSSEAU THE EDUCATIONAL THEORIST

Rousseau's revolutionary point of view. 1. Introduction: Education must be determined by the spontaneous interests and activities of the child and be guided by the development of the child.

2. The Old Position is False: The old idea that the child's education is to be governed by adult interests and activities

is false. This old idea leads to untruths. The Child is a Little Adult. This is false, for the child is an individual wholly different from the adult. Thus, education is not the acquiring of what adults wish, but is furnishing the child with the proper environment for growth in terms of his true inner nature. The Interests of Society are Above Those of the Individual. This is false, for it means the crushing of the individuality of a child. The individual is a precious entity that is to be bent to no outer will. The needs and interests of the individual are above those of organized society. The Child's Nature is Unimportant. This is false, for all true education is based upon understanding of the nature of children and their environment.

3. The Recapitulation Theory: In the individual's development from childhood to adulthood he lives again each epoch in the history of civilization. These stages are definite and clear, sharply marked from each other: Animal stage (from birth to five). Savage stage (from five to twelve) when self-consciousness emerges. Rational stage (from twelve to puberty) when the rational faculty emerges and the higher sentiments develop. Social stage (from puberty to adulthood) when sex emerges and social relations properly begin. Here also religious life properly develops. Each stage is a complete unit of development and does not lead on to the next. The education of the child is not preparation for adult life. At each stage the child is to be taught what is useful for him at that stage only.

Rousseau's educational aims. His fundamental aim was preservation of man's natural goodness and creation of a society which would insure its most complete development. Rousseau conceived a form of education for an ideal state organized in accord with the nature of man with education a public function and available to every child. Its aim is to foster natural virtues and a sense of social unity. This ideal is developed in his *Discourse on Political Economy, The Social Contract,* and *Considerations on the Government of Poland.* He also conceived a form of education for a society such as his own. Here education must protect the child from the evils of society until he is able to protect himself. This is developed in *Emile.* Here education is for the higher classes and aims at a generous, liberal cultivation of the child's natural endowments and avoids specialization. It seeks to fit the child for a changing environment. Since we do not know the future, we must educate in terms of the child's present needs. If this is well done, he will be able to meet the future adequately.

Rousseau's educational institutions. 1. Public Education: Rousseau favored public education that leads to social unity and a sense of equality. This leads to nationalism.

2. Family Education: The family educates in cooperation with the state. This is the Calvinistic position. Education should begin with the family and later be taken over by the state.

3. The Isolation of Emile: This is education of the wealthy boy who is to be educated as a savage to enter society as it is. He must be protected until he is able to resist successfully the society of his day.

The stages of man's growth. 1. Infancy (from birth to five) : This stage is concerned with growth of the body, motor activities, and the beginnings of sense perception and feeling. Here one should follow the methods of nature. The child's individuality must be respected. He must be freed from restraint, but his body must be hardened by nature's methods. The adult must permit the child to become self-dependent. During this period the child's education consists of the free and unhampered expression of his natural activities in relation to his physical environment. The child should be permitted to act naturally and to experience directly the results of his actions.

2. Childhood (from five to twelve): Rousseau criticized the methods used by schools of his day at this level. He held that the concentration upon books was wrong and he would eliminate books and expose the child to things. Education must be negative—"do nothing and allow nothing to be done." Let the child develop as his inner nature demands and protect him from outer interference. The child cannot reason. Thus, experience is his only teacher. He learns through necessity directed by his natural development. The curriculum at this level should consist of natural activities. The child will pick up reading incidentally; he will learn his mother tongue naturally; he will develop his organs, senses, and powers.

3. The Age of Reason (from twelve to fifteen): At this age reason emerges. The child's strength has outrun his needs and reason emerges as a "check to strength." Here education by human agencies begins. They direct the unfolding process. We must not try to educate the child through reason; we must not use authority in place of the child's mental efforts, but help him to make his reason the authority; and we must not make the mistake of thinking that reason is the driving power of life. The motivating factors at this level are the desire to learn (curiosity) and the usefulness of knowledge (utility). The curriculum at this level is drawn from *Robinson Crusoe* and consists of exercising the intelligence in the world of nature—geography, astronomy, physical sciences, agriculture, manual arts, and crafts. Rousseau was not concerned so much with learning material as with the acquiring of a correct method of thought, a desire for knowledge, and clear and accurate ideas. Nothing is to be learned from the authority of others but rather through

experience, by direct observation and discovery. The child should make all his own materials for a study.

4. Social Stage (from fifteen to twenty) : Here sex emerges and with it the social urge. This is the period when perception of human relations, appreciation of beauty, the sense of moral and social life, religion, and the higher virtues awaken in the child. Sex demands a companion, and human relationships become dominant. Here the youth studies psychology, sociology, ethics in concrete life situations. Natural religion emerges.

Rousseau's theory of the education of girls. In this he contradicts all he has advocated for Emile. The girl is educated to please the man and everything that she is to learn is relative to men.

S. E. FROST

CONTENTS

ROUSSEAU ON EDUCATION

INTRODUCTION

I.—Nature of his Influence.

As the French Revolution, which was largely an attempt
to carry out Rousseau's political theories, marks the
beginning of the modern period in political history, so
the *Émile* may be said to have inaugurated a new era in
the history of education. This does not mean that
modern States are based on the *Social Contract* or
modern education on the *Émile*. Indeed, the reader who
opens the latter book for the first time and sees its
paradoxes, its exaggerations, and its obvious absurdities,
cannot imagine it capable of forming the basis of any
educational system. What, then, is meant when it is
said that without the *Social Contract* and without the
Émile the politics and the education of the last century
must have followed an entirely different course?

In estimating the effect of the French Revolution, we
take into account—(1) Its destructive work in removing
long-standing obstacles to reform; (2) its effect in
removing the mere *vis inertiæ* which was perhaps more
serious than any more positive obstacle; (3) the stimulus
which it afforded to innovators of various countries and
various opinions; (4) the necessity which it imposed on

existing institutions to justify their existence by reform; and (5) even the negative effect of rousing the champions of opposite ideas to show their advantages, and to realize the best of which they were capable. For example, the stimulus which was given to the sentiment of nationality by the attempt of the revolutionaries to sweep away national distinctions may be fairly counted among the negative effects of the Revolution.

Rousseau's influence on education must be judged similarly. We should not limit our attention to such of his views as have come to be recognized as correct; we should take account of his influence under each of these five headings:

1. European education in Rousseau's time consisted of the moribund forms of two, if not three, great intellectual movements; foremost, of the Renaissance, which had made Greek and Latin literature the basis of culture; secondly, of the scientific discoveries of the seventeenth century, which had created a demand for smatterings of encyclopædic information; while, thirdly, there were still to be found, mingled with the newer strata, outcrops of mediæval Scholasticism, chiefly in the form of logic and ethics. Rousseau attacked the system on every side— aims and results; physical training, moral training, and intellectual training; curriculum, methods, and discipline. It was based on a theory that men were born bad, whereas they were born good.[1] Physically, it tried to keep children from risks; they could only grow up healthy by running risks.[2] It knew but two means of moral training—punishment and preaching—both of which ruined character.[3] Of the intellectual systems, that of the Renaissance taught how words might be used to conceal the absence of thought;[4] encyclopædism

---

[1] Pp. 55, 84.   [2] Pp. 63, 64.   [3] Pp. 95-98.   [4] Pp. 110-112.

loaded a child's memory with facts which he could neither use nor understand;[1] logic and ethics combined the evils of both.[2] Since Rousseau's time, willingness to go to first principles and to reject existing practices which could not be justified thereby has become possible.

2. Rousseau appeared at a time of educational stagnation. The seventeenth century had been hopeful of reform. In the eighteenth, even those who would not have agreed with Dr. Johnson that "the last word on education had been said long ago," had lost the faith of earlier periods in its possibilities. After Rousseau optimism once more prevailed. Novelty was no longer regarded with suspicion; indeed it was almost too popular. Once more men began to believe that, if education had accomplished little, the fact was due not to any inherent limitations in its possibilities, but to the kind of education that had been tried.

3. The stimulus exercised by Rousseau roused educational reformers of a more practical type. Pestalozzi's interest in education was directly due to him. Froebel took his principle of following the child's nature—that is, his instincts—and worked it out into the Kindergarten method. Even Herbart would probably not have written on education but for the same stimulus, though in his case we are approaching the influence by reaction. It may be noticed that nowhere was the effect of Rousseau's stimulus more effective than in elementary education, though he himself considered that the children of the poor stood in no need of schooling.[3]

4. If the new movements of the following period were due to Rousseau, so also was the revival of existing agencies. The revived faith in education led to the

[1] Pp. 109, 114.   [2] Pp. 176-177.   [3] P. 71.

great reform of the secondary school system of Prussia
in the first years of the new century; while twenty or
thirty years later the English public schools emerged
from a storm of criticism, having shaken off their chief
abuses and developed their strong points.

5. It is worthy of note that in these two instances the
reactive effect predominates. Both produced a high
form of a literary education; the English schools
developed the corporate spirit more than had been
previously known. In regard both to the value of
literature as an educational instrument, and to the
facilities which a school affords for a training in corporate life, the right theory had been expressed for
centuries before Rousseau; the former was a common-
place of the Renaissance writers, and the latter was
urged by all who supported a school training against
private tuition. But practice had belied theory. When,
however, Rousseau wished to remove books from education till fifteen,[1] and denied that children were capable
of social relations, then the whole energies of education
were turned to disproving him by practice. Herbart's
work may be primarily regarded as a psychological and
practical attempt to justify a literary education; while
the work of Arnold of Rugby was largely an attempt to
stem the tide of moral anarchy which was to his mind
the propelling force of the French Revolution.

It is no paradox to assert that Rousseau's power lay
in his limitations. Men who see all sides of a case are
not revolutionaries; had Rousseau not been a revolutionary, he would at that period have been ineffective.
What was needed was a man who could feel more
intensely than others the evils which others saw or
were ready to see, and one who could make them believe

---

[1] Pp. 119, 162.

that these evils could be swept away in favour of a new system by a short, sharp, and decisive revolution. Few reforms would be carried if the mass of their supporters realized at the beginning how slow and difficult a process reform is. Rousseau not only believed in the possibility of rapid reform; he believed in it irrationally, violently, obstinately. The force of his emotions carried others with him. Moreover, his manner of writing was particularly suited to lull to sleep their critical powers. His political and educational theories always appear to be based on axiomatic first principles, and to be deduced from them by the most obvious and irrefragable logic. This specious appearance is maintained even when he is running counter to general experience, and when he is in reality influenced in his conclusions mainly by his prejudices. His rhetorical power also enabled him to appear to be entering into the minutest detail while he is really omitting to notice serious practical difficulties.[1] This double power of exciting enthusiasm and inducing an abeyance of the critical faculties is often shown by a speaker, rarely by a writer. Where it is exercised, we have the contagious influence of a mob which carries away its individual members. Rousseau by his pen made the French public into such a mob, and the contagious influence did not die away in education till it had affected the whole of the civilized Western world.

II.—MODE OF STUDYING ROUSSEAU.

These considerations determine our attitude in reading Rousseau. If we approach him as an authority, even if

---

[1] *E.g.*, he enters into great detail as to the Latin and Greek authors which Émile should read, but fails to tell us how he is to acquire the necessary knowledge of the languages.

we read him mainly to find the sound principles, neglect-
ing the unsound, we shall be disappointed. It does not
follow that a study of his works is valueless. The value
is twofold : first, existing opinions, like existing institutions, are most clearly understood when we have traced
their origin; secondly, something is always to be learned
from the views of opponents. A study of Rousseau
serves both purposes; in one sense he is the earliest of
modern educationalists; yet from another he is the most
thorough-going opponent of modern education.

Education is relative to the period; it must change as
knowledge enlarges, as ideals change, as the needs of
society change. The best education of the fifteenth and
sixteenth centuries is not the best for the twentieth.
But changes in education often lag behind the changes
in social ideals. If reform has been long delayed, then
there must follow a comparatively rapid readjustment.
Such periods of readjustment are the most important
in studying the history of education. The conflict
between the new and the old sets in clear relief the
ideas which underlie the education of the new period.
What are the ideas which Rousseau attacks as outworn,
why does he so regard them, what are his new ideals,
are they truly the ideals of the nineteenth century, how
far have they in their turn been superseded, how far
have they grown and developed ? The answer to these
questions gives us the basis on which the education of
the present day must be built.

Such is the way of reading Rousseau from the historical
standpoint. But he may also be regarded as a critic of
modern education, whose views may be suggestive even
where they cannot be accepted. For many of the ideals,
and still more of the practices, against which he declaimed
hold their own to-day; in many cases, as has been already

pointed out, the chief effect of his writing was to lead to a revival of the ideals which he attacked. Modern education aims at educating the citizen; it trains the future member of the economic body for a place in an industrial system which is far more complex than any of which Rousseau dreamed; it strives to instil into the child of Western Europe traditions or, as Rousseau would hold, the prejudices of twenty-five centuries of European civilization; it uses literature as its main instrument in this task; it takes as its watchward progress, which is the departure from "Nature.". Fundamental principles are often obscure till they are attacked; if the attack is not insidious, but open, daring, asking for no compromises and holding them to be impossible, recognizing that such as are the aims so must be the means—and this was the character of Rousseau's attack —then the study of the opponent will do more than anything else to clarify our perception of the bases of the system which is attacked and to strengthen our hold upon them.

But the study of Rousseau must be critical—that is, we must keep our attention fixed on the premises, not be content to enjoy the rhetorical unrolling of the conclusions. His ideas of society, his moral ideal, his psychological assumptions are clearly enough stated; his conclusions are stated equally clearly; but it is for the reader to see how far errors in the premises vitiate the conclusions.

A short attempt must now be made to show the origin of Rousseau's most characteristic views.

III.—Origin of his Views.

He himself tells us that his political and educational views form one complete whole.[1] He also describes how these views were formed. There is no reason to doubt the substantial accuracy of this account. Two incidents in his career were mainly instrumental in determining the flow of his thoughts. His youthful wanderings brought him into contact with the French peasant and convinced him that French society rested on a wrong basis. The question propounded for a prize essay by the Academy of Dijon, whether the progress of the arts had contributed to human happiness, suggested to him the further stage in his thought that modern civilization was not wrong merely by accident but in virtue of its inherent character as civilization. He describes his state of mind as he revolved the problem in terms which would appropriately describe a sudden conversion. Ideas surged before him with a force and clearness which seemed super-normal. There formed in his mind the basis of the scheme which was later given to the world in his written works. In interpreting the working of Rousseau's thoughts, we have to remember that we are dealing with a man so susceptible to the power of an *idée fixe* that, in his prime, his passion for "Julie" amounted almost to madness, and, in later life, the idea of a conspiracy to persecute him is thought by many to have definitely passed the bounds of sanity. We may therefore assume that from the time of his "conversion"

---

[1] P. 23. The two early discourses represent the basis of his political views, and the *Émile* of his views on education. The *Social Contract* had not then been written; but it is merely an elaboration of views expressed in a digression in the *Émile* and in the earlier works.

his ideas possessed such a hold over his mind as to exclude all opposing or modifying considerations, that they exercised an emotional power which is rarely experienced in the case of intellectual and abstract conceptions, and that they occupied his whole mind with a kind of delirious force which would not let him rest until they had been expressed.

The fanatical hold of his views upon his mind was, however, largely concealed from him by the fact that the elements of which they were composed were by no means original. The novelty consisted in the combination. The political theory which had been worked out since Hobbes and the antagonism of the Illumination to authority were to that age the expression of the best recent thought. He might well consider that he was but uniting these two elements and the accepted psychology in one logical whole. The reader recognises that in addition to these three elements, the result is coloured by ethical ideals resulting from Rousseau's own character; but of this he was probably unconscious. A brief consideration must be given to each of these four components.

The " State of Nature," which was invented by stress of logical requirements to justify a political theory, had been stated by its authors and accepted by educated opinion as if it were an historical fact. French society under Louis XIV. and English society of the " Augustan period," jaded with superficiality and deceived by exaggerated accounts of the virtues of American Indians, had elevated this imaginary era into a Golden Age. Rousseau, more daringly consistent and less instinctively sane than his predecessors, took them at their word, and asked men to return to it. The views that man is not originally or by nature a " political (or social) creature," that men become social only through the pressure of their individual needs,[1] that their young are therefore born unsocial,[2] that instincts or virtues which are apparently social are only self-regarding instincts metamorphosed,[3] and that the child of to-day can best be induced to enter the social state by the same considerations as drove his savage ancestors into it,[4] are all either different ways of stating the doctrine of the " State of Nature " or obvious corollaries from it.

Rousseau's psychology is substantially that which had come down from the days of Aristotle. Mental activities were assigned to certain supposed " faculties," each of which developed at a particular period of life. This view played havoc with all attempts to present a theory of education up to the nineteenth century.[5] If its results are more startling in Rousseau than in his predecessors, it is because he possessed in a remarkable degree the characteristically French capacity for seeing all the consequences which can be deduced from a general proposition, while he was singularly lacking in the knowledge that results are rarely produced by the operation of single causes, which is impressed on every student of science and on every practical man. Rousseau was constantly led astray by the deductive method. Reason and the social emotions must each arise at a definite period ; he took twelve and fifteen as the respective ages ; and, assuming that a boy is irrational till twelve and unsocial to fifteen, he will not allow him to be acquainted with anything which involves the use of reason or social feelings till these ages. Hence the postponement of most of the ordinary school subjects.[6]

---

[1] Pp. 183, 189.   [2] P. 141.   [3] P. 181.   [4] P. 163
[5] *E.g.*, Comenius's system is entirely based on it.
[6] Pp. 108-115.

He failed to see the paradox that we only become rational by reasoning and only acquire social feelings by social action.[1]

The third source of Rousseau's views has been stated as the opposition to authority which formed the basis of the Illumination, against which in some respects he started a reaction. Apart from authority, the only bases of belief and social conduct are reason and social instinct. Whatever is taught of belief and social conduct before the age at which reason and social instinct develop is dependent on authority, and therefore bad.[2] Premature teaching on these matters was not merely useless; it was positively harmful; it was instilling prejudices which would afterwards check the action of reason.[3] The boy was to be left free, when reason appeared, to follow it as freely as if he had no existence till that age. The earlier education must not therefore inculcate virtues, but it must prevent the growth of vices.[4] It was to be negative. Absolute plasticity at the birth of reason was his goal.

But throughout the logical development of these principles on which Rousseau was consciously working, we can trace the factor of Rousseau's own character determining the shape of the finished product without his knowledge. It affects both his ideal and the means of attaining it.

Rousseau was intensely introspective, and his standard of perfection was obtained mainly by omitting elements from his own character, and idealizing what was left. He recognized some of his positive vices; he failed to recognize the absence of virtues. This is most marked in regard to self-control, which he implicitly assumes to be impossible. In his own case the existence of a bad

[1] P. 147. [2] P. 94. [3] Pp. 195, 196, 202, 203. [4] P. 107.

impulse meant its triumph. Hence he throws his whole
energy into the impossible task of securing that his
pupil shall never be subjected to temptation either
from without or from within; and entirely neglects the
strengthening of character which would enable him to
resist it. In reading the *Émile*, we sometimes feel that
Rousseau is pleading at the bar of his own conscience,
"Not guilty; for no man is ever guilty, the fault is
always with circumstances." Such an attitude means
moral suicide. The failure to recognize the existence
of virtues which he did not possess comes out again in
his confusion of humanitarian sentimentality with a
working altruism. The whole treatment of the training
of Émile's behaviour to others is based on this fallacy.[1]
Self-sacrifice is not trained so easily.

Furthermore, Rousseau's introspective habit caused
him to think his fellow-men to be more like himself
than they really are. When he recognizes a fault
in himself, he overestimates the liability of mankind at
large to it. Vanity and jealousy[2] were among his
signal vices; instead of tracing them to his own isolation, he tries to guard against them by elaborate and
unnatural precautions.[3] Hence competition, which after
all is a law of life, is not to be moralized, but to be
eliminated.[4] Again, fear lest the pupil should follow
the unhappy bent of the immoral passions which ruined
Rousseau's own happiness runs through the whole of the
fourth book of the *Émile*.[5] Thus the personal element
influenced his views as to what boys and men actually
are as well as his ideal of what they should be.

In this statement of the underlying assumptions of
Rousseau, the reader will have noticed that we have

[1] Pp. 183, 188.   [2] P. 156.   [3] Pp. 182, 197.
[4] Pp. 97, 126   [5] P. 204

been dealing with two quite different kinds of principles, with views as to facts, and views as to values. His theory of the historical origin of the State and his psychology deal with questions of fact; and, if his opinions are untrue, the chief importance of seeing their effect on the sum total of his theory is in order that we may eliminate the element due to them, and see how what remains is dependent on estimates of value. Rousseau stands for extreme Individualism against the claims of society; he stands as an opponent of authority, and as the upholder of a certain ideal of character, and, in particular, he lays little stress on self-control. A profitable study of his work can therefore be made if the reader puts his own views on these matters clearly before his mind, and sees how his difference from Rousseau in regard to the premises will lead to differences in the conclusions. A further point of view would be to consider how far Rousseau's direct influence is still affecting modern thought and practice under the various headings, and, if so, whether that influence is in accordance with the reader's own conclusions or otherwise.[1] It is of the highest value to bring to light the latent presuppositions which lie at the base of tendencies of the present day.

IV.—ALLEGED CONTRADICTIONS IN ROUSSEAU.

Some doubt has been cast on the extent to which Rousseau held some of his more startling principles by comparisons of the *Émile* with his other works. These

---

[1] To take the most obvious instance, it is often held that there is a tendency abroad never to make children do what is disagreeable. How far can traces be found of such a feeling of a kind to suggest that it is based on a spread of Rousseau's ideal of character?

concern chiefly—(1) the impossibility of educating the child as a citizen; (2) the absence of family life; and (3) the purely negative character of early education—in fact, the most characteristic parts of the *Émile*. In the following extracts the apparently contradictory passages have been given[1] as far as possible. The first is the most difficult problem; but the *Émile* itself approves of the civic education of antiquity. The most probable conclusion is that, if Rousseau could have found a State after his heart—and he looked for it in Poland, Corsica, etc.—like many who uphold toleration while they are a minority and become persecutors when they come to be a majority, he would go to the opposite extreme. His attitude is that education must be wholly civic or wholly individualistic.[2] This answer, however, only raises further difficulties; for what becomes of Rousseau's opposition to Authority, his psychology, and his following of Nature? Is loyalty to the perfect State to override these? In regard to the second difficulty, there is one passage at least in the *Émile* extolling the family.[3] As the purpose of this edition is to give the author's words and leave the reader to form his own conclusions, it is not wise to embark on a discussion of these difficulties, which could not possibly be confined to a brief space.

V.—EXTENT OF ROUSSEAU'S INFLUENCE.

The points which Rousseau chiefly emphasizes in his letters of practical advice, and which had the greatest

---

[1] For (1) see extract in the *Government of Poland*, pp. 64-69; (2) and (8) the ideal family life in the *Nouvelle Héloïse*, which involves a vast amount of direct personal influence.

[2] P. 58.   [3] Pp. 72, 75.

influence upon his contemporaries, were not so much
the views which are peculiar to him, as such unexcep-
tionable points as these : personal care of parents for
their children's education, consistency of treatment,
absence of the personal element in punishment, greater
liberty in play, avoidance of "spoiling," precautions
against the obsequiousness of servants and the flatteries
of visitors, and, above all, good example.

The general character of his influence on succeeding
generations has already been discussed. It remains to
specify a few of his principal positive views, which have
been accepted either generally or by some considerable
party.

His most widely accepted views are those which concern
training through activity, mental or bodily. The following propositions were all more or less spread by his
influence : (1) Intellectual knowledge is only properly
grasped when the mind has worked with it ;[1] (2) interest
in intellectual knowledge is aided by physical application of it ;[2] (3) handicrafts—as opposed to branches of
science—can be used to foster intellectual activity;[3]
(4) physical exercise, games, and handicrafts give a
sense-training, which in turn reacts on intellectual
work ;[4] (5) manual activities create a habit of thinking
about the world's work which the pure scholar lacks ;[5]
(6) in hand-work children will be more interested if they
are allowed to aim at results from the first, pure technique being introduced gradually as the children see the
need for it.[6] In his enthusiasm for a handicraft Rousseau
was, however, greatly influenced by his impracticable

[1] Pp. 175-177.   [2] P. 158.   [3] P. 172.   [4] P. 127.
[5] P. 169.
[6] It is strange that this principle is only now beginning to be
acted on. Herbert Spencer has probably forced its recognition
in Great Britain.

ideal of economic independence—that everyone should be able to do everything for himself so as to avoid being dependent on others.[1] This is, of course, diametrically opposed to the principle that the division of labour makes for economic advance, and takes away one of the great aids to morality—the recognition that we are " members one of another."

Other influences which have been traced to Rousseau are—(1) the milder treatment of children, especially the total disappearance of the idea of " breaking their wills," which is sometimes alleged to be due to Rousseau's view that children are born good,[2] not bad as the theologians said; (2) the heuristic idea; (3) discipline by natural consequences. The growing humanity of the nineteenth century may, however, be assigned to a variety of causes;[3] and Rousseau's heuristic idea is very different from Professor Armstrong's, as it aims at training practical versatility, not the spirit of scientific research.[4] The third influence is probably really Rousseau's; for, though Herbert Spencer had not read the *Émile*[5] when he revived it, the idea had probably filtered through to him by indirect channels.

Finally Rousseau is often credited with having introduced a radically new idea into education in the shape of " following Nature,"[6] which has since been developed. Apart from other senses in which he and all other educational writers since Aristotle have used this ambiguous

---

[1] Pp. 169, 170.   [2] P. 55.

[3] Mr. Holmes has again put forward the view that the doctrine of the corruption of human nature tends to repressive discipline. Comenius in theory and the Port Royalists in practice suggest that it may produce an exactly opposite result. After all, may not Mr. Holmes's complaints suggest the truth of the doctrine—as applied to teachers ?

[4] Pp. 157, 158.   [5] Pp. 103-105.

[6] *E.g.*, Monroe, *History of Education*, chap. x.

and much abused phrase, this is taken to mean the nature of the child. It is therefore important to notice that Rousseau is rather the climax of the pre-evolutionists, while Froebel, though he wrote long before Darwin, is the first of the evolutionists. As long as instinctive tendencies (with which we must identify Nature, if it is to have any precise meaning)[1] were regarded as divine gifts instituted as a perpetual and infallible guide to behaviour, it was possible to "follow" them—that is, to give them opportunities for growth without directing them.[2] But, as soon as they are seen to have grown up to fit man for a more primitive environment, it becomes clear that they must be modified. Froebel's system *uses* them to the full, but it does not *follow* them. Education is their master, not their slave.

VI.—NOTE ON THE ESTIMATE OF ROUSSEAU'S CHARACTER.

The publication of Mrs. Macdonald's startling defence of Rousseau against many of the charges which have been commonly accepted for the last hundred years may appear to necessitate a revised estimate of his character. In so far as his character is a factor in determining the origin of his educational theories, this is not really the case. Indeed, the fact that ingratitude, treachery, and double-dealing, the faults of which Mrs. Macdonald has acquitted him, do not appear to colour his theories, while vanity, jealousy, absence of self-control, and sexual passion appear in strong relief, is a strong confirmation of Mrs. Macdonald's discoveries. In other words, Rousseau unconsciously betrays, by his precautions in the educa-

[1] P. 57.
[2] The orthodox view of the imperfection of human nature prevented this view from being widely adopted.

tion of Émile, just those vices of which he deliberately pronounces himself guilty, while there is no unconscious trace of those other faults of which he has been accused by his enemies only. Mrs. Macdonald's theory as to his alleged treatment of his children does not affect our view; whether his children ever existed, or were sent to the Foundling Hospital or not, is immaterial; his belief in the truth of the common story is the essential fact. In either case, the passages in the Émile[1] may be regarded as the result of remorse and of a wish to deter other parents from adopting such a course. The only point where it is possible that modification is necessary is in attributing such strength to Rousseau's morbid and introspective tendencies as to make them pass the bounds of sanity. Assuming the truth of Mrs. Macdonald's evidence, the most natural interpretation appears to be that Rousseau's persecutors knew of the existence of these tendencies, that to some extent they were a contributing cause of their dislike of him, and that with diabolic ingenuity they used them as instruments in the mental torture with which they carried on their persecution.

[1] Pp. 14, 15.

NOTE

The text includes a translation of between one-quarter and one-third of the *Émile*, Rousseau's formal educational treatise. An attempt has been made to preserve continuity; and this task is rendered easier by the large number of digressions and repetitions in Rousseau's writings. The whole of the Savoyard Curate's Confession of Faith in Book IV. has been omitted; and of the second half of Book V., only a very few extracts and a summary are given. About half of the first three books is translated; here the omissions more frequently consist of repetitions than of continuous passages. Throughout, omissions of sections are indicated; as also of sentences or paragraphs, except in a few passages where a note has been added to show that the passage has been greatly condensed. This occurs chiefly in some of the illustrative anecdotes. The extracts from *Émile* make up about three-quarters of the present volume. The other quarter consists of (1) a long passage from the *Nouvelle Héloïse*, which may be regarded as his first draft of his educational theories; (2) of a letter to the Duke of Würtemberg on the education of his daughter and several shorter letters, which are given to show how far Rousseau modified his views to meet concrete circumstances; and (3) a passage from the treatise on the Government of Poland, which must necessarily be presented to enable the reader to see the reverse side of his views on the relation of education and citizenship.

The translation of the *Émile*, published by Donaldson in 1768, the only complete English translation, has been consulted, but has been so modified that the present translation is practically new. The same holds true of a companion translation of the *Nouvelle Héloïse*. The translations of the minor works are original.

I

INTRODUCTORY

a. LETTER TO M. DE MALESHERBES (January 12, 1762).

[This letter may serve as an introduction by Rousseau himself to his educational works.]

It may appear impossible to combine in the same individual an indolent disposition which shirks trouble and an impulsive choleric temperament which is easily affected and is over-sensitive to everything which affects it; yet these contradictory principles form the basis of my character. Though I give no theoretical explanation of this combination, it nevertheless exists; I feel it, nothing is more certain, and I can at least give some facts in my history which may serve to make it comprehensible. In childhood I had unusual energy, but not that of the normal child. Tedium drove me at an early age to books. At six I happened to light on Plutarch; at eight I knew him by heart; I had read all the romances; they had drawn from me floods of tears before the age when the heart has awakened to an interest in romance. From this source sprang my taste for the heroic and romantic, which has never ceased growing ¡to the present time, and has ended by blunting my taste for everything which does not resemble my day-dreams. In my youth, when I expected to find in the world the characters whom I had known in books, I surrendered myself unreservedly to all who could impose on me by a jargon of which I had always been the dupe. I was active because I was infatuated; in proportion as I was disillusioned, I changed my tastes, my attachments, and my projects; in all my changes I was perpetually wasting time and energy, for I was perpetually looking for something which had no existence. With experience I had almost lost the hope of finding it, and therefore the energy to look for it. Soured by the unjust treatment which I had received and witnessed, I despised my generation and my contemporaries: feeling that I had never found among them a situation which could satisfy my heart, I had gradually withdrawn myself from the society of men and constructed a new society in my imagination, which pleased me all the more because I could develop it without trouble or risk, and could find it always sure and satisfying.

After passing forty years of my life discontented with myself and others, it was in vain that I struggled to break the bonds which bound me to a society which I esteemed so little. It held me bound to distasteful occupations by needs which I believed to be inspired by Nature, though in truth they were but the work of opinion. Suddenly a happy chance revealed to me how I ought to act for myself, and what I ought to think of my fellow-men. Indeed, my heart had always been at variance with my understanding; for I had constantly been impelled to love my fellows, though I had so many reasons for hating them. I will try to describe to you the moment which constituted so strange an epoch in my life: however long I live, it will still be present to my mind.

I had just been to see Diderot, at that time a prisoner at Vincennes. I had in my pocket a copy of the *Mercure de France,* which I started reading as I walked. My eye fell on the subject set for an essay by the Dijon Academy, which was the occasion of my first attempt at writing. If anything ever resembled a sudden inspiration, it was the feelings which I experienced on reading this announcement; I felt suddenly dazzled by flashes of illumination; crowds of clear ideas came to me in a moment, with a confusing force which left me inexpressibly troubled; my brain seemed dazed, like that of a drunken man. . . . Could I ever have written a quarter of what I then saw and felt, how clearly should I have revealed the contradictions of the social system! with what force I should have exposed the abuses of our institutions! with what ease I should have shown that man is naturally good and only becomes bad through our institutions! All that I could retain of that host of all-important truths which revealed themselves to me in that quarter of an hour has been feebly scattered through my three principal works: The *First Discourse,* the *Discourse on Inequality,* and the *Treatise on Education.* The three works are inseparable, and together form one whole. The rest has all been lost; there only remains besides the *Prosopopée de Fabricius.* That is how, when I was least thinking of such a career, I became an author, almost in spite of myself.

b. CONDITIONS ASSUMED IN *ÉMILE.*

[From Book I.]

I formerly made an attempt to perform this work (*i.e.,* that of a tutor). It was enough to convince me that I am not fitted for it. . . . Unable to undertake the more useful task, I shall venture to attempt the easier; following the example of others, I shall not set my hand to the work, but to the pen; and, instead of doing the work myself, I shall endeavour to teach others what it is which ought to be done. . . .

I have, therefore, in this treatise made choice or an imaginary pupil and taken the liberty to suppose myself of the right age, in good health, and possessed of the requisite knowledge and abilities to undertake his education, to conduct him from the time of his birth till he is grown to maturity, and no longer stands in need of any other guide than himself. . . .

I shall not here speak of the qualifications of a good tutor, but assume that I possess them. In reading the treatise the reader will see how liberal I have been to myself. I shall only observe—

[1. That the tutor should be "as young as is consistent with having attained the necessary discretion," because "there are not enough things in common between childhood and manhood to form a solid attachment at so great a distance."

2. That they continue together from infancy to manhood.

Emilé is assumed to be a wealthy orphan. "It is to no purpose that he should have parents. As I charge myself with their obligations, I succeed to their rights."]

[To show that Rousseau regarded it as essential that the complete time of a tutor should be devoted to a single pupil, apart from the exigencies of the book, the following letter is given :]

c. LETTER TO M. D'EYBENS (1740).

M. de Mably asks the terms on which I can take charge of the education of his sons. . . . What troubles me most is the fear that the number of pupils may spoil my work. It would be desirable that I should not be obliged to divide my attention between so many; the most attentive of men finds it difficult, in the case of only a single pupil, to enter into all the details which must be considered to make sure of a good education. I admire the happy readiness of those who can train large numbers at the same time, but I dare not promise that I can do likewise. But I can promise this, that I will spare no pains to succeed. In regard to the eldest, I know him to be of so promising a temperament that I am already convinced that he will not leave my hands without being my equal in feeling and my superior in knowledge. This is not much to promise; but I must limit my undertakings by my capacities; the rest depends on the boy himself.

II

EXTRACT FROM "JULIE" OR "LA NOUVELLE HÉLOÏSE"

[*Julie*, published in 1761, is a romance told by means of a series of letters written by the different characters. In one of these letters Rousseau takes the opportunity of presenting an ideal picture of the education of children by wise parents. Julie, Madame de Wolmar, is describing her system to the writer of the letter. He urges the popular view, but is ultimately convinced.]

I.—DIFFERENCE OF CHILDREN AND ADULTS; ABSENCE OF REASON.

"I SEE," I said, "that heaven rewards the virtue of mothers by the good disposition of their children: but a good disposition needs training. Their education ought to begin from birth. Can any time be better fitted to train them than that early period when there are no impressions to be effaced? If you let them follow their own inclinations from childhood, at what period will you expect them to learn obedience? Surely it is best to teach them to obey you at a time when you have nothing else to teach them."

"Have you noticed," was the reply, "that they disobey me?"

"That would be difficult," I answered, "when you never command them."

She looked at her husband and smiled; then she took me by the hand and led me into her boudoir where we three could continue the conversation out of hearing of the children. Here she explained her principles at leisure; and, under her apparent negligence, I discovered the most watchful attention which a mother's love could possibly bestow.

"For a long time," she said, "I used to agree with you about beginning early. When I was expecting my first child, I was alarmed at the idea of my impending duties, and I often spoke of them to M. de Wolmar with anxiety. What better guide could I take in such a matter than an enlightened observer who combined the interest of a father with the impartiality of a philosopher? He exceeded my expectations. He scattered my prejudices and taught me how, with less trouble, to secure a far greater success. He made me realize that the earliest and most important education is precisely that which is universally neglected; it is to put a child in a position to be educated. A general mistake amongst parents who pride themselves on being intellectual is to imagine that children are rational beings from their birth and to talk to them as if they were grown up, even before they can talk. Reason is regarded as an instrument to instruct them; whereas all the other means of instruction should be treated as instruments to develop their reason. Reason is of all the human powers the latest and the most difficult to train. In speaking to them so early in a language which they do not understand, we accustom them to be satisfied with words, to pay others in the same coin, to cavil at everything which is said to them, to think themselves as wise as their masters, and to become argumentative and captious. Further, everything which we think we are obtaining of them by reasonable motives is really gained only by the motives of fear or vanity which we are always obliged to unite with the former. The most consummate patience ends by giving up a child whom we try to educate in this manner : that is how it comes to pass that parents, tired, disheartened, and exhausted with the unceasing restlessness for which they are themselves responsible, and unable to bear the noise of their children any longer, are obliged to hand them over to tutors, as if it were to be expected that a tutor would have a greater stock of patience and kindness than could be possessed by a father."

"Nature," continued Julie, "means children to be children before they become men. If we deviate from this order, we produce a forced fruit, without taste, maturity, or power of lasting; we make young philosophers and old children. Childhood has ways of seeing, thinking, and feeling peculiar to itself. Nothing is more foolish than to wish to substitute our own; I would sooner expect a child to be five feet in height than to be able to reason at ten years of age.

"Reason begins to develop only after some years, when the body has reached a certain stage of development. Nature's intention is to strengthen the body before exercising the mind. Children are always in motion; quiet and meditation are their aversion; a studious or sedentary life is injurious to their health and growth; neither their minds nor their bodies can bear constraint. Always confined in a room with books, they lose all their vigour; they become frail, delicate, and unhealthy, stupid rather than reasonable: their minds suffer all their lives from the enfeeblement of their bodies."

II.—No Mistakes in Nature; Individuality.

" Even if all this premature instruction were as good
for their minds as it is actually harmful, it would still be
a great mistake to bestow it on all children indiscriminately and without regard to their individual
differences.   Apart from general human characteristics,
each individual is born with a distinctive temperament
which determines his genius and character.   There is no
question of changing or restricting this temperament,
only of training it and bringing it to perfection.   All
characters (according to M. de Wolmar) are good and
healthy in themselves.   There are no mistakes, he says,
in nature ; all the faults which we impute to innate
disposition are the effect of the bad training which it
has received.   There is no criminal whose tendencies,
had they been better directed, would not have produced
great virtues.   There is no failure in whom useful
talents could not have been developed if he had been
given the right bias, just as deformed and monstrous
figures are rendered beautiful and well-proportioned by
placing them in the proper position from which to view
them.   Everything tends to the common good in the
general scheme.   Every man has his special place in the
ideal order of the universe ; it is a question of finding
out his place, not of changing the universe.   What
results from an education begun from the cradle and
always carried out on the same system without regard
to the extraordinary differences between human minds ?
The effect is usually to give children harmful or mis-
placed instruction, while they are deprived of the
teaching which would really have suited them.   Their
nature is confined on every side ; great qualities of
mind are destroyed to make room for small, apparent,

unreal substitutes. We indiscriminately employ children of different bents on the same exercises; the rest of their education destroys the special bent, and the result is a dull uniformity. Then after we have wasted our efforts in stunting the true gifts of nature, we see the short-lived and illusory brilliance which we have substituted die away, while the natural abilities which we have crushed never revive. We lose both what we have destroyed and what we have put in its place; and at last, as the reward of our ill-directed labours, we find these little prodigies all becoming men without power or merit, noticeable only for their uselessness and their weakness."

"I understand these maxims," I said to Julie, "but I can scarcely make them agree with your own opinions as to the small advantage which comes from developing the genius and natural talents of each individual, either for his own happiness or for the true good of society. Would it not be infinitely better to form a perfect model of a reasonable and virtuous man and to mould every child according to this model by means of education? We should stimulate one and restrain another; we should check their passions, perfect their reason, correct their nature——"

"Correct nature," said Wolmar, interrupting me—"a fine phrase! But, before using it, you ought to reply to what Julie has just said."

The most direct reply seemed to be a denial of the principle; I accordingly denied it. "You always assume that this difference of minds and of capacities which marks individuals is the work of nature; this is not at all clear. For, if minds are different, they must be unequal; and, if nature has made them unequal, it must be by giving to some either a little greater delicacy of sense-perception, or a little greater power of memory, or a little greater capacity for attention. Now, as regards the two former, the senses and the memory, it is proved by experience that their different degrees of range and accuracy are not the measure of men's higher mental powers; and, as regards the third, power of attention, it depends entirely on the strength of the passions which inspire us. It has further been proved that men are by nature universally capable of passions sufficiently strong to arouse that degree of attention which is required for mental superiority. But, if mental differences, instead of arising from nature, are an effect of education—that is to say, of the different ideas and feelings which are aroused in us from childhood, by the objects which meet our senses, by the circumstances in which we are placed, and by all the impressions which we receive—then, so far from postponing education till we know the character of our children's minds, we ought to take the earliest opportunity to create the right character by means of an education directed to that end."

To this he replied that it was not his way to deny what he saw because he could not explain it. " Look at those two dogs in the court; they are from the same litter, they have been fed and treated in the same way, they have never been separated; yet one of them is lively, brisk, friendly, and intelligent; the other is dull, heavy, bad-tempered, and never able to understand anything. Difference of innate disposition is solely responsible for the difference in their characters; similarly in men, difference of internal organization is solely responsible for difference in mental powers; all the rest has been just the same."

" The same!" I interrupted—" rather, how different!

How many trifling objects have influenced the one and not the other! how many small circumstances have affected them differently without our noticing it!"

"Good!" he replied, "there you go, arguing like the astrologers. Whenever they are faced with the argument that two men born under the same horoscope have such different fortunes, they totally deny the identity. They contend that, considering the rapid movement of the sky, there is really an immense distance between the themes of the two men and that, if we could mark the exact moment of their respective births, the objection would be changed into a proof. Let us give up, I pray you, all these subtilties, and confine ourselves to observation. It informs us, indeed, that there are some characters which are obvious almost from birth and some children who can be studied in their nurse's arms. These constitute a class apart; they are being educated from the moment of birth. But the rest develop less quickly. By trying to train their minds before we understand them, we risk spoiling the good qualities of nature and putting worse in their place. Did not your master Plato maintain that all human knowledge and all philosophy could not extract from a human soul anything which nature had not placed in it, just as all the operations of chemistry can never obtain from an alloy more gold than it contains? This does not apply either to sentiments or to ideas; but it applies to our capacity for acquiring them. To change the mind, you must change the interior organization; to change the character, you must change the temperament on which it depends. Have you ever heard of a hot-tempered man becoming phlegmatic or of a cold methodical mind becoming imaginative? For my own part, I am convinced that it would be as easy to change a blonde into a brunette as a

fool into a man of genius. It is in vain then to claim
that we can model different minds by a common
standard. We can dwarf them, but not change them;
we can hinder men from showing what they are, but we
cannot make them otherwise; and if they wear their
disguise in the ordinary course of their life, you will, on
all important occasions, see them resume their original
character, and surrender themselves to it with all the less
restraint, because they are not aware of its existence.
Once more, it is no question of changing the character or
bending the natural inclinations, but, on the contrary, of
expanding them as far as they will go, of training them
and not permitting them to degenerate; for it is thus
that a man becomes all that he is able to be and that the
work of nature is completed by education. Thus, before
developing character, we must study it; we must wait
quietly till it reveals itself and refrain from all action
rather than act amiss. One temperament needs to be
given wings, another to be confined in fetters; one needs
encouragement, another restraint; one commendation,
another threats; some we must enlighten, some keep in
ignorance. This man is meant to attain the utmost
bounds of human knowledge; to another it is dangerous
even to learn to read. Let us wait for the first spark of
reason to bring out the character and show its true
form. Only in the light of this knowledge can we train
the character; before the appearance of reason there is
no true education.

"As regards the maxims of Julie which you consider
contradictory, I do not know where you see the contradiction; for my own part, I find them perfectly compatible. Every man is born with a character, abilities,
and talents peculiar to him. Those who are destined to
live in rural simplicity have no need, in order to be

happy, to develop these faculties; their talents lie buried
like the gold-mines of the Valais, which it is forbidden
in the public interest to work. But in the civil state,
where there is less need of arms than of brains, and
where everyone must render an account of all his talents
both to himself and to others, we must learn to draw
out of men all that nature has implanted in them; we
must incline them in that direction where they will be
able to develop furthest; above all we must provide
their inclinations with that kind of nutriment which will
render them useful. In the case of the rustic we think
only of the class; each member does the same as the
rest; example is their only rule, habit their only power;
each of them exerts only that part of his mind which is
common to all. In the case of men living in civilized
communities, we think of the individuals; we add to
each everything that he can possess over and above
that possessed by his fellows; we let him go as far as
nature will take him; if he has the requisite qualities,
he may become the greatest man alive. So little are
these maxims contradictory that their application to
childhood is identical. Do not teach the village child,
because it is not in his interest to learn at all. Do not
teach the town child, because you do not know *what*
teaching will be to his interest. In both cases leave the
body to develop till the dawn of reason; then train the
reason."

III.—LIBERTY; NEITHER SUBJECTION NOR COMMAND.

" Your plan," I said, " would appear to me excellent,
did I not see one defect which seriously detracts from
its expected advantages. It is that you allow a crop of
bad habits to grow by not occupying the ground with
good. Look at children who are left to themselves;

they soon contract all the faults of which they see examples. Bad examples are easy to follow; they never imitate virtuous conduct, which it costs more to practise. Accustomed to get everything which they want and invariably to carry out their foolish purposes, they become fractious, headstrong, and ungovernable."

"But," replied M. de Wolmar, "you seem to have noticed a different result in the case of our children; indeed, it was that which gave rise to the present conversation."

"I admit it," I answered; "that is the reason for my surprise. What has madame done to make them tractable? How has she gained a hold over them? What has she substituted for the yoke of discipline?"

"A yoke far more unyielding," he cried instantly, "that of necessity. But she will make you understand her views better if she describes her procedure." He then asked his wife to explain her method. After a short pause she began:

"The secret of happiness is a good disposition. I do not lay so much stress on our training as my husband. In spite of his theories, I doubt whether you can get good results from a bad character, and whether every disposition can be turned to good. Otherwise I am convinced of the excellence of his method, and invariably try to conform to it in the management of my family. My first prayer is that I may never have a bad child, my second that I may so bring up the children whom God has given me under their father's direction that they may one day have the happiness of resembling him. I have therefore tried to carry out the rules which he has laid down; but I have given them a basis less philosophic and more agreeable to a mother's love—to make my children happy. This was my first prayer

when I became a mother, and my efforts are perpetually
directed to its fulfilment. When I took my first child
in my arms, I reflected that childhood is almost a quarter
of the longest life. We rarely reach the remaining three-
quarters; and it is cruel forethought to sacrifice the happiness of this first portion to that of a remainder which
will perhaps never be ours. I felt that nature subjects
poor helpless children to so many restrictions that it is
cruelty to impress a further restraint by our caprices
and to take from them the little liberty which they
possess and which they have so few opportunities to
misuse. I resolved to spare my own all the restraint
I could, to leave him complete freedom to use his scanty
powers and not to thwart any of his natural inclinations.
By this course I have already gained two great advantages: one, that I have saved his young mind from
deceit, vanity, anger, and jealousy, from all the vices,
in short, which result from slavery and which we cannot
avoid instilling in our efforts to enforce obedience; the
second, that I let his body grow freely with the constant
exercise to which his instincts prompt him. He is accustomed, just like a country child, to run bare-headed
in sun and frost, to get out of breath, and to throw himself into a perspiration; and so he grows hardened, like
the country child, to the weather, and becomes stronger
as well as happier. This is the way to provide for
maturity and to insure against the accidents to which
we are all subject. As I have already told you, I am
afraid of this fatal anxiety which enervates and enfeebles
a child by constant precautions, torments him with constant constraint, enslaves him with a host of useless
safeguards, and eventually exposes him all his life to
those inevitable dangers from which it is anxious for the
moment to preserve him; which, in order to save him

a few colds in childhood, lays up for him in the future consumption, pleurisy, sunstroke, death.

"The real reason why children who are left to their own inclinations generally contract the faults which you mention are that they are not content with doing as they like themselves, but they further try to make others fall in with their wishes. This tendency is encouraged by the foolish indulgence of mothers; they are not satisfied unless everyone falls in with their children's fancies. I flatter myself, my friend, that you have never noticed in my children a trace of domination or authority over the lowest servant, that you have never seen me secretly encourage the false servility which servants tend to show towards children. This is where I think that I am following a new and safe road to make my children at once free, quiet, affectionate, and obedient. It is a very simple plan; it consists merely in convincing them that they are only children.

"We have only to think of the condition of childhood. Is there any creature in the world weaker, more unprotected, more at the mercy of its surroundings, more in need of pity, of love and of protection, than a child? Is not this the reason why the first sounds which nature prompts are cries and laments, why she has given him so sweet and touching an appearance, that all who approach him may sympathize with his frailty and hasten to his assistance? What, then, can be more shocking, more unnatural, than to see a domineering refractory child commanding everything around him, shamelessly assuming the tones of master over those who have only to leave him to himself to cause his death, and to see blind parents approving of this audacity and training him to be a tyrant over his nurse until he comes to exercise his tyranny over themselves?

"For my part, I have spared no pains to prevent my son from acquiring these dangerous ideas of dominion and slavery. I never allow him to think that he is served as a matter of right, but from pity. This is, perhaps, the most important and difficult point in education; and it would take too long to recount all the precautions which I was obliged to take to prevent them from distinguishing by a ready instinct between the mercenary services of domestics and the tenderness of a mother's love.

" One of the chief means which I have used has been, as I have said, thoroughly to convince him how impossible it is that a child of his age should live without our help. After I had done this, I had no difficulty in making him feel that all the assistance which he was obliged to receive from others was a sign of dependence, and that the servants had a real superiority over him. He could not do without their help, but he renders them no service in return. And so far from being proud of their services, he receives them with a sort of humiliation, as evidence of his weakness; he ardently longs for the time when he will be big and strong enough to have the honour of serving himself."

"These notions," I said, "would be hard to establish in households where the father and mother are themselves waited on like children; but in this family, where each, beginning with yourselves, has his own duties to perform, and where the relations of servant and master is merely a perpetual interchange of needs and services, I do not think it impossible. Nevertheless, I do not see why, if children are accustomed to see their real wants anticipated, they do not expect the same gratification of their fancies; or why they do not sometimes suffer from the mistake of a servant who treats a real need as a case of fancy."

IV.—CONTROL: RELATIONS OF PARENTS TO CHILD.

"My friend," answered Madame de Wolmar, "an ignorant mother will see difficulties in everything. The true needs both of children and of men are very few. Moreover, we should be more concerned for permanent than for monetary happiness. Do you think that a child who is under no restraint and is under his mother's eyes can suffer any real harm from the mistake of a governess? Your objections presume that faults have already been contracted, and you forget that my previous precautions have prevented their growth. Women naturally love children. Misunderstanding only arises between them when one side wishes to subject the other to its caprices. But this cannot happen in our case : nothing is demanded of the child, and the child has no occasion to command the governess. I have thus acted directly contrary to other mothers, who pretended to wish the child to obey the governess, but really wish the governess to obey the child. Here no one either commands or obeys; the child merely obtains from others the same kindness which he feels for them. His knowledge that his only influence over those about him consists in their good-will makes him tractable and obliging ; in trying to win the hearts of others, he becomes attached to them in turn. In seeking to be loved, one comes to love ; love is an inevitable outcome of self-interest: and from this mutual affection—the result of equality—spring without effort all the virtues which our constant homilies fail to secure. . . .

"The indulgence which is lavished on young people from their birth, the consideration which everyone displays for them, the ease with which they obtain their desires, cause them to enter the world with the foolish prejudice that everything should yield to their fancies, and they are often disillusioned only by humiliations, affronts, and suffering. I wish to save my son this second and mortifying education; and this can only be if his first education, which he receives from me, gives him a truer view of life. I had at first resolved to give him everything which he asked, under the belief that the first promptings of nature are always good and healthy. But I was not long in seeing that children who think that they have a right to be obeyed abandon the state of nature almost at birth; they contract our vices from our example and their own from our indiscretion. I saw that, if I tried to satisfy all his fancies, these fancies would increase with my indulgence, that there must come a point at which I should be compelled to stop, and that he would then take a refusal to heart all the more because he was unaccustomed to it. I could not save him all disappointment before he reached the age of reason; so I chose the least and most transient form. Since a single refusal involves the least cruelty, I determined to refuse at once; and, in order to spare him long unhappiness, complaint, and waywardness, to make every refusal irrevocable. It is true that I refuse as little as possible and think twice before refusing at all. Whenever I grant his requests, I grant them without conditions and as soon as he asks; and we grant them freely. But he never obtains a request by importunity —tears and wheedling are equally useless. He knows this so well that he no longer tries: at the first word he understands his position, and he is no more unhappy when we take away a box of sweets which he would like to eat than at the escape of a bird which he would like to catch. He classes both enjoyments as impossible. If anything is taken from him, he merely considers it impossible that he should keep it; if a request is refused, he merely thinks it impossible that he should obtain it: and, so far from beating a table against which he had hurt himself, he would not beat a person who resisted him. In all his disappointments he sees the power of necessity and the result of his own weakness, never the effect of the ill-will of others. One moment," she added a little hurriedly, as she saw that I was going to reply, "I foresee your objection; I shall come to it in a moment.

"The cause of children's ill-temper is the attention which we pay to it; and this is the same whether we grant or refuse their requests. If they once see that we do not want them to cry, they will cry the whole day. The means which we take to quiet them, whether coaxing or threatening, are equally harmful and nearly always ineffective. So long as we notice their tears, they have a reason for continuing; when they see that no one minds them they will soon improve; for no one, old or young, cares to take useless pains. That is exactly what happened with my elder boy. At first he was always crying; he used to stun the whole household; now, as you can see, no one could tell that there was a child in the house. He cries when he is in pain; that is the voice of nature which should never be silenced; but he stops crying the moment the pain is over. I pay great attention to his tears, because I am sure he never sheds them for nothing. Thus I know at any moment whether he is or is not in pain, and whether he is well or ill; that is impossible with children who cry from caprice and merely in order to be coaxed. I quite admit that it is difficult to induce nurses and governesses to adopt this plan; for nothing is more wearisome than to hear a child always crying, and, as these good women never look beyond the present, they overlook the fact that by quieting the child to-day they are making him cry more to-morrow. But the worst result is the formation of an obstinate habit, which will continue for years. The same cause which makes him fretful at three makes him refractory at twelve, quarrelsome at twenty, tyrannical at thirty, and unbearable all his life.

"I now come to your point," she said, smiling. "Whenever you grant children's requests they easily see your wish to please them; whenever you exact anything from them or refuse a request, they ought to imagine that you have reasons without asking what they are. This is another advantage which you gain by using authority rather than persuasion where one or the other is necessary: for as they cannot fail sometimes to see the reasons for our treatment, it is natural for them to imagine that we have a reason even when they cannot see it. If, on the contrary, you have once submitted your actions to their judgment, they claim the right to judge it on all occasions; they become argumentative, crafty, prevaricating, and underhand, always trying to silence those who are weak enough to expose themselves to their ignorance. If you are compelled to explain to them things which they cannot understand, they attribute the most rational conduct, if it is above their comprehension, to caprice. In a word, the only way to make them submit to reason is never to reason with them, but thoroughly to convince them that reasoning is beyond their powers: they will then suppose it to be on the side where it should be, unless, indeed, you give them strong grounds for thinking otherwise. If they are sure that you love them, they know very well that you do not wish to cause them unhappiness; and children are rarely deceived on that point. When, therefore, I refuse any request of my children, I do not argue with them, I do not tell them why I am unwilling to grant it, but I find ways, as far as is possible, to let them discover the reason, sometimes after the event. In this way they become accustomed to understand that I never refuse a request without a good reason, although they cannot always discover it.

" On the same principle I shall never allow my children to join in the conversation of reasonable people, and foolishly imagine that they are on an equality with them because they tolerate their silly prattle. I wish them to answer briefly and modestly when they are asked questions, but never to speak till they are spoken to, and particularly not to ask foolish questions of their elders whom they ought to respect."

"Truly, Julie," I interrupted, " these are rigorous rules for so kind a mother. Pythagoras was not your equal in strictness to his disciples. It is not only that you do not treat them as men ; one would think that you are afraid of their ceasing too soon to be children. What can be a more pleasant and a surer means of learning, if they are ignorant, than questioning those who know ? What would the Parisian ladies think of your maxims ? They never think that their children can prattle too much or too long ; they regard their childish nonsense as a token of mature genius. Of course your husband would say that this suited a country in which fluent speech is the highest recommendation ; where, if a man can talk, he is excused from thinking. But how can *you*, with your anxiety to make your children happy, reconcile happiness with so much restraint ? And, with all these restrictions, what becomes of the liberty which you claim to leave them ?"

" What !" she replied instantly, " is their own liberty

restricted by our preventing them from trespassing on ours? Can they not be happy unless the whole company is silently admiring their prattle. Prevent the appearance of vanity, or at least arrest its course; that is really working for their happiness! Vanity is the source of men's greatest troubles, and there is no one so great or so admired that vanity has not caused him more pain than pleasure.

"What can a child possibly think of himself when he sees around him a whole circle of sensible people listening to him, encouraging him, admiring him, waiting with tense impatience for the oracles that fall from his lips, and breaking out in raptures at each silliness he utters? Such false applause is enough to turn the head of an adult; think what effect it will have on a child! . . .

"With regard to questions, I do not forbid them indiscriminately. I am the first to tell them (if they need to know anything) to ask quietly, especially of their father or myself. But I do not allow them to interrupt a serious conversation and to trouble everyone with the first trifle which comes into their heads. The art of asking questions is not so easy as is thought. It is rather the art of a master than of a pupil. You must already know much to be able to inquire about what you do not know. The wise know and inquire, says an Indian proverb, but the ignorant know not even what to ask. For want of this previous knowledge, the questions of children who are allowed to ask indiscriminately are either foolish and purposeless, or else are hard and ticklish inquiries to which the answer is beyond their comprehension. That is the reason why they generally learn more from the questions which they are asked than from those which they ask themselves.

"But let us suppose that the contrary method were as

good as is commonly supposed. Still is not the first and most important lesson at their time of life to be reserved and modest, and should they learn any other to the detriment of this ? What, after all, do children gain by this freedom of speech almost before they can talk ? by this right of audaciously subjecting others to cross-examination ? They are converted into babbling little inquisitors, questioning less for information than to attract notice and to make everyone attend to them; their loquacity is further encouraged by the obvious embarrassment which their indiscreet questions cause, till at last everyone is uneasy as soon as they open their mouths. It has little effect in teaching them, but much in making them vain and conceited; and, in my opinion, the disadvantage greatly outweighs the advantage. Ignorance is bound to diminish, vanity can only increase.

"The worst that could happen from too prolonged a reserve would be that, when my son reached years of discretion, his conversation would be less fluent, his discourse less lively and ready : but, when we reflect how seriously the understanding is impoverished by this habit of devoting our lives to mere words, I am tempted to regard this happy limitation as a blessing rather than as a misfortune. Idle people, who are always bored, naturally attach great value to anything which will amuse them : but one would think that the art of pleasing consisted in making no remarks which were not silly and in giving no presents except those which are useless. But human society has a nobler object; its real pleasures are more substantial. The organ of truth, the most worthy organ that man possesses, by which alone he is distinguished from the animals, was not given him to serve no better use than do their inarticulate cries. He degrades himself below them when he uses speech to say nothing; and man ought to be man even in his moments of relaxation. . . .

"But it is a far cry from six to twenty. My boy will not always be a child, and in proportion as his understanding ripens, his father intends that he shall be allowed to exercise it. My part does not extend so far. I nurse children but I am not presumptuous enough to wish to train men. I hope," she added, looking at her husband, "that more worthy hands will be charged with this noble task. I am a woman and a mother, and I know how to keep my proper sphere. I repeat, the duty with which I am charged is not the education of my sons but to prepare them to be educated.

"In this I only follow point by point the system of M. de Wolmar; and the further I progress the more I realize how sound and excellent a system it is and how well it agrees with my own. Look at my children, especially the eldest; have you ever seen children more happy, gayer, less troublesome? You see them jumping, laughing, running about all day, without ever causing trouble to anyone. Is there any pleasure, any liberty, which children of their age could enjoy, which they do not possess? Is there any which they misuse? They are as little constrained in my sight as in my absence. On the contrary, they always seem more at liberty under their mother's eye; though I am responsible for all the severity which they undergo, they always find me far from severe; for I cannot bear the thought of not being the dearest object to them in the world.

"The only rules which we impose on them in our company are the essential rules of liberty—to lay the company under no greater restraint than it lays on them, not to shout louder than we talk, and, as we do not compel them to take notice of us, not to compel us to notice them. If they break these rules, their only punishment is to be sent away at once, and my one means of making this a punishment is to see that they like no other place so well. Otherwise they are under no restrictions; we never compel them to learn a lesson; we never weary them with useless corrections; we never reprimand them; the only instruction they receive is the simple instruction of experience, in which we follow nature. Everyone in the house, being well instructed on the point, conforms to my instructions with an intelligence and care which leave nothing to be desired; and if any failure *were* to be feared, my own care would easily prevent it or set it right.

"Yesterday, for example, the eldest boy, having taken a drum from his brother, made him cry. Fanny said nothing; but an hour afterwards, when she saw him in the height of his amusement, she took it from him. It was now his turn to cry. He followed her, asking her to give it back. Her only reply was: 'You took it from your brother and I am taking it from you. What have you to say? Surely I am stronger than you.' Then she began to beat the drum as if for amusement, just as he had been doing—so far, excellent; but later on she was going to give the drum back to the younger boy. Then I stopped her; this was no longer one of nature's lessons, and might sow the first seeds of jealousy between the two brothers. In losing the drum, the younger submitted to the hard law of necessity; the elder felt his injustice, and both knew their weakness and were happy a moment afterwards."

V.—LEARNING.

A plan so novel and so contrary to received ideas at first surprised me. By dint of explanation, however, they ended by winning my adherence, and I felt convinced that the path of nature is always man's best guide. The only disadvantage which I could see in the method—and it seemed a serious flaw—was its neglect of the only faculty which children possess in perfection, a faculty which can only grow weaker with the advance of years. I felt that, according to their own system, the feebler and more inadequate are the operations of the understanding, the more we ought to exercise and strengthen the memory, which is so capable at that age of standing strain. "Memory," I said, "should supply the place of reason before it appears and enrich it after its appearance. If the mind has no exercise, it becomes dull and heavy by inaction. The seed takes no root in untilled soil; and it is a strange manner of preparing children to become reasonable to begin by making them stupid."

"How! stupid!" cried Madame de Wolmar at once. "Would you confuse two qualities so different, almost opposite, as memory and judgment? As if the mass of ill-digested and disconnected information with which we load the frail brains of children did not do more harm than good to the understanding. I admit that of all the faculties of the human mind memory is the first to appear and the most suitable to train in childhood; but which in your opinion is to be preferred, that which is easiest to learn or that which is most important to know? Consider the use which is generally made of this aptitude, the violent treatment to which they must submit, and the constant constraint to which they must be subjected in order to store their memory; and then compare the usefulness of the result with the sufferings which they undergo during the process. Fancy compelling a child to study languages which he will never speak, even before he has learned his own! making him incessantly repeat and compose verses which he does not understand and whose metre is merely a trick of the pen! confusing his mind with circles and spheres of which he has not the least idea! burdening him with a hundred names of towns and rivers, which he constantly confuses and is obliged to re-learn every day! Is this training the memory for the benefit of the understanding? Are these trifling acquisitions worth one of the tears which they have cost him?

"If uselessness were the most serious charge that could be brought against such a system, I should not complain so strongly. But is it a small thing to teach a child to be content with words, to believe that he knows what he cannot even understand? Will not this lumber block the entry to the earliest ideas with which we should furnish the human mind? Better no memory than one filled with rubbish to the exclusion of that needful knowledge of which it takes the place!

"If Nature has given (*vide* p. 114). . . .

"Do not think, however," continued Julie, "that we altogether neglect that training which you value so highly. If a mother is the least watchful, she has the passions of her children under her complete control. She has means of arousing and sustaining the desire to learn or any other desire; and, so far as they are compatible with the complete freedom of the child and do not sow the seeds of vice, I readily employ them. But I am not the least perturbed if they are not attended with success; there will always be time to learn; but there

is not a moment to be lost in forming the disposition.
M. de Wolmar, indeed, lays such stress on the first
dawnings of reason that he maintains that, though his
son knew nothing at the age of twelve, he would know
not a whit less at fifteen; and, even if it be otherwise,
yet there is not the least need for a man to be a scholar,
but nothing is more needful for him than to be wise
and good.

"You know that our eldest boy already reads tolerably
well. His wish to read arose thus. I proposed occasionally
to recite to him some of La Fontaine's fables for his
amusement; and I had already begun when he asked
me if ravens could talk. In a moment I felt the difficulty of making him understand the difference between
a fable and a falsehood; I got out of the difficulty as
best I could and laid aside La Fontaine, convinced that
fables are made for men but that plain truth must be
told to children. I substituted a collection of instructive
and interesting little stories, mainly taken from the
Bible; and, finding that he grew interested, I conceived
the idea that it would be still more useful if I myself
tried to compose a series, which should not only amuse
but also be appropriate to the needs of the moment.
These I wrote out in a bold hand in a handsome picture-
book, which I always kept locked up. Now and again
I read some of these stories, but not often, and never
for long at a time; and I frequently repeated the same
story with comments before passing on to the next. A
child left idle is soon bored, and the little stories were
a great resource. When I saw him particularly absorbed,
I sometimes pretended to recollect an order about dinner
and, carelessly putting the book down, left him at the
most interesting point. He would at once run to ask
his nurse or Fanny or someone to begin reading; but,

as no one is at his command and all had their instructions, no one ever complied. One refused, another was busy, a third muttered slowly and unintelligibly; while a fourth, following my example, left off in the middle of a story. As soon as we saw that he was thoroughly tired of depending on others, someone privately suggested to him that he should learn to read, and thus set himself free and be able to turn over the pages at pleasure. He was delighted with the proposal. But he must find someone kind enough to teach him. This was a new difficulty, which we took care not to make too great. In spite of all these precautions, he grew tired of learning three or four times; but we took no notice. All I did was to try to make my stories still more entertaining : he returned to the attack with so much enthusiasm that, though it is not six months since he began to learn, he will soon be able to read the whole collection for himself.

"This is the way by which I shall try to arouse his zeal and inclination to acquire all such knowledge as needs continuous application and is suitable to his age. Though he is learning to read, it is not from books that he will gain information; there is no such thing in the books he reads, nor is reading a suitable means for children to acquire knowledge. I am anxious to train him at an early age to stock his head with ideas and not with words; and that is the reason why I never make him learn anything by heart."

"Never !" I interrupted, "that is going very far. Surely he must learn his catechism and his prayers."

"You are wrong," she replied. "As regards prayers, every night and morning I say mine aloud in my children's room : in this way they learn them without any compulsion ; as for the catechism, they have never heard of it."

"What! Julie, your children do not know their catechism?"

"No, my friend, my children do not know their catechism."

"Indeed!" I said in complete astonishment, "with such a religious mother. I cannot understand you. Why do they not learn it?"

"That they may believe it one day," was the reply: "I wish my children some day to be Christians."

"Ah! I see," cried I; "you do not wish that their belief should consist merely of words; you wish them not only to know their religion but to believe it: and you hold rightly that a man cannot believe what he does not understand. . . ."

VI.—CONCLUSION.

After entering into other details which convinced me how active, how indefatigable and foreseeing was her maternal zeal, she concluded by remarking that her method exactly answered the two purposes which she had set before her, that is, to allow her children's natural disposition to develop, and to study it.

"My children are under no restraint in anything," she continued, "yet they cannot misuse their liberty. Their character can neither be constrained nor perverted. Their bodies are left to grow and their judgments to ripen in peace. Their minds are not debased by servitude. Self-love is never kindled by the attentions of others. They never think themselves either powerful men or caged animals, but free and happy children. To guard them from vices which are foreign to their nature, they have what seems to me a better safeguard than lectures which they will not understand or from which they will turn with disgust, and that is a virtuous example in all which surrounds them—in the conversations which are natural to everyone here and do not need to be specially prepared for them, in the peace and concord which they see, and in the harmony which they always observe both between the conduct of different people and between everyone's conduct and his conversation.

"Brought up hitherto in their natural simplicity, whence should they contract vices of which they have never seen an example, passions which they have no occasion to feel, and prejudices with which there is nothing to inspire them? You see that they are the prey of no delusion and manifest no bad inclination. Their ignorance is not opinionated; their desires are not obstinate; their inclinations to evil are anticipated; Nature is justified, and everything serves to convince me that the faults of which we accuse her are not hers but our own.

"Thus, given up to the inclinations of their own hearts without disguise or alteration, our children are not cast in an external and artificial mould, but preserve the exact form of their original disposition. Thus it comes to pass that this disposition daily unfolds itself to our gaze without reserve and gives us an opportunity of watching the workings of nature, even in their most secret springs. Sure of never being scolded or punished, they do not know how to lie or to deceive; and whatever they say, whether to us or to each other, they reveal without reserve what lies at the bottom of their hearts. Free to prattle to one another all day, they are not for a moment restrained by my presence. I never check them nor bid them hold their tongues nor pretend to listen to them; and, though they should say the most reprehensible things, I should never appear to notice them.

I am, however, really listening with the greatest attention, though they do not know it; I keep a most exact
record of their acts and words; for I recognize in them
the natural products of a soil which I have to cultivate.
Vicious conversation in their mouths resembles a weed
whose seed has been carried by the wind : if I cut it off
with a scolding, it will soon grow again; I prefer to look
for the hidden root and carefully to pull it up. " I am
only," she added with a smile, " the gardener's help; I
weed the garden and pluck up the tares; the gardener
must cultivate the good seed.

" Let us agree too that, with all the care I have been
able to take, I must be well supported if I am to hope for
success, and that the issue of my cares depends on a
combination of circumstances which can perhaps be
found only here : the knowledge of an enlightened father
is needed, amid existing prejudices, to discover the true
art of bringing up children from birth; all his patience
must be devoted to carrying it out, without ever contradicting his lessons by his behaviour; the children must
be blessed by Nature with a good innate disposition that
we may love her work; and they must have around them
only intelligent and well-disposed servants, who will not
fail to enter into their master's designs. A single brutal
or servile domestic may spoil everything. In truth,
when I think how many external causes may ruin the
best plans and overthrow the wisest projects, I ought to
thank fortune for her goodness and to confess that
wisdom is at the mercy of chance."

III

INTRODUCTORY PASSAGES FROM THE "ÉMILE," WITH PARALLEL PASSAGES

1. EDUCATION AND NATURE.

Opening of the *Émile*.

EVERYTHING is good as it comes from the hands of the Creator; everything degenerates in the hands of man. He compels one soil to nourish the products of another and one tree to bear the fruits of another; he mingles and confounds elements, climates, and seasons; he mutilates his horses, dogs, and slaves; he defaces everything, he reverses everything; he delights in deformity and in monsters. He is not content with anything as Nature made it, not even his fellow-man. Even his offspring must be trained up for him like a horse in his stable, and must grow after his fancy like a tree in his garden.

Indeed, matters would be still worse if it were otherwise; for our species cannot be civilized by halves. In the existing order, a man who, in the midst of his fellow-beings, was left from birth to his own resources, would become more unnatural than they all; prejudice, authority, necessity, example, all those social institutions by which we are surrounded would stifle in him the emotions of nature without substituting anything in their place. He would resemble a shrub which chance had set in a public highway—kicked and pulled out of shape by every passer-by.

Tender and provident mothers, prudent enough to leave the beaten track and to preserve this growing shrub from the shocks of human prejudice, to such are my words addressed! Cultivate, water the young plant ere it die; it will one day bear fruit delicious to your taste. Set up a fence betimes round your child's soul; others may mark its circuit, but you must build the barrier.

Plants are formed by cultivation, men by education. Should a man come into the world in full maturity and vigour, his size and strength would be useless till he had learned how to use them; they would, indeed, be prejudicial, by preventing others from thinking that he needed help. Left to himself, he would die before he learned his needs.

We are born weak, we need strength; we are born entirely destitute, we need help; we are born stupid, we need understanding. All that we lack at birth and need in maturity is given us by education.

This education we receive from three sources—Nature, men, and things. The spontaneous development of our organs and faculties constitutes the education of Nature, the use to which we are taught to put this development constitutes that given us by men, and the acquirement of personal experience from surrounding objects constitutes that of things.

Each of us is therefore educated by three kinds of masters. The pupil in whom their lessons are contradictory is badly educated and will never be consistent. Only where they are perfectly consonant and make for the same ends, does a man tend towards his true goal and live consistently. Only thus is he well educated.

Of these three kinds of education, that of Nature is not under our control, nor, except in certain respects, is that of things; the education given by men is alone in any true sense within our power, and even this only in theory; for who can hope to exercise a minute control over the words and deeds of all who surround a child? As soon as education becomes an art, it is almost impossible that it should succeed, as the conditions necessary to its success are not within the control of any one person. All that can be done by our efforts is to approach more or less closely to our end; we must trust to fortune whether we reach it.

If it be asked what is this end, it may be answered, That of Nature. This has just been proved. For, since the concurrence of the three kinds of education is necessary to their completeness, the kind which is entirely independent of our control must necessarily regulate us in determining the two others.

But perhaps this word "Nature" may appear too vague; we must therefore endeavour to define it.

Nature, it has been said, is only habit. But to what purpose is this said? Do we not know of habits—contracted merely through compulsion—which can never suppress the tendency of nature? Such a case occurs when plants are prevented from growing upwards. Take off the restraint; though the twist remains, the rise of the sap has not altered, and, if the tree continues to grow, the growth will be once more upwards.

It is the same with inclinations imposed on men. As long as conditions remain unchanged we may retain even the most unnatural habits; but with a change of circumstances the habit loses its power and nature reasserts itself. Education is certainly nothing but habit; but is it not true that some persons lose its impressions while others retain them? Whence arises this difference? Nature means more than the habits to which Nature will submit; otherwise we might be spared this discussion.

We are born with a capacity for receiving sensations; from our birth we are affected in various ways by surrounding objects. As soon as we acquire what I may call an awareness of our sensations, we are disposed to pursue or to avoid the objects which produce them. At first this is dependent on their pleasant or painful quality; later, on the congruity or incongruity which we discover between the objects and ourselves; and finally on our estimate of them in the light of the ideas of happiness or perfection given us by reason. These tendencies are extended and strengthened with the growth of knowledge and discrimination; but they are also subject to the constraint of habit, and are consequently more or less modified by our opinions. I use the term 'nature' to refer to these tendencies as they exist prior to this modification.

2. EDUCATION AND THE STATE.

a. Émile (continuation of last passage).

To these original dispositions we ought always to go back. This would be possible if the three kinds of education were merely different; but what can be done seeing that they are opposed? If, instead of educating a man for himself, we wish to educate him for others, the concurrent action of the three kinds becomes impossible; we are forced to contradict either nature or the institutions of society. We must therefore choose whether we will make a man or a citizen; we cannot do both.

Every narrower society, if it be truly coherent, is thereby alienated from the wider society, which is mankind. The true patriot is unfriendly to foreigners; they are only men, they are nothing to him. This result is inevitable, but it is not serious. The essential point is that a man should be useful to those among whom he lives. Abroad, the Spartan was ambitious, covetous, and unjust; but disinterestedness, equity, and concord reigned within his walls. Always distrust those cosmopolitans who preach obligations to mankind and neglect to practise them towards their neighbours. Such a philosopher loves the Tartars as an excuse for not loving his own people.

The natural man has a value in his own right; he is a numerical unit, an absolute integer, and has no relation but to himself and to his fellow-man. Civilized man is only a relative unit, the numerator of a fraction, that depends on its denominator, and whose value consists in its relation to the integral body of society. The best political institutions are those which are most calculated to divest men of their natural being, to substitute a relative for an absolute existence and to swallow up the individual in the social unity. A citizen of Rome was neither Gaius nor Lucius, but a Roman; he loved his country, though he must thereby hate himself. Regulus declared himself a Carthaginian, on the ground that he had become the property of his captors. As an alien, he refused to take his seat in the Roman Senate till he was commanded by a Carthaginian. He was indignant that they wished to save his life. He persuaded the Senate, and as a result of his success returned to perish by torture. Such conduct has little relation, I think, to the men whom we know to-day.

The Lacedæmonian Pædaretes presented himself for

election to the Council of Three Hundred and was rejected; he returned home rejoicing that there were to be found in Sparta three hundred men more suitable than himself. Supposing his demonstrations of joy to have been sincere, as there is room to believe they were —there you see the true citizen.

A Spartan woman had five sons in the army and was awaiting news of the battle. An islander arrives. Trembling, she asks him the news. "Your five sons are killed." "Vile slave, who asked you of my sons?" "But we have gained the victory." The mother rushes to the temple to give thanks to the gods. There you see the woman as citizen.

Those who wish to retain in the social order the primitive sentiments of nature do not know what they ask. Ever contradicting himself, ever wavering between duty and inclination, he will be neither man nor citizen; he will be good for nothing either to himself or to others. He will be *the modern man*, an Englishman, a Frenchman, a *bourgeois*; he will be—nothing.

To be something, to be himself, to be always the same, he must act as he speaks: he must ever be clear as to the part he is to take; he must accept it whole-heartedly and cling to it unceasingly. I must wait till I am shown such a prodigy before I can tell whether he is man or citizen, or how he manages to be both at once.

From these aims, opposed by their very nature, arise two opposite kinds of education, the one public and general, the other private and particular.

To form an idea of public education, read Plato's *Republic*. It is not a system of politics, as is imagined by those who judge of books only by their titles; it is the finest treatise on education ever written. When we wish to suggest a realm of chimeras, we often mention the training of Plato. Had Lycurgus laid down his system only in writing, I should have thought it a much greater chimera. Plato only refines the human heart, Lycurgus altogether changes it.

Public education no longer exists nor can exist; for where is no country, there can be no citizens. The words *country* and *citizen* should no longer find a place in our modern tongues. I could give my reasons, but I omit them as irrelevant to my subject.

I do not count as public training those ridiculous establishments called colleges.[1] Nor do I count the lessons of the world, because it aims at two contradictory ends and falls short of both. It serves only to make men deceitful, always appearing to care for others, while they never really care for anything but themselves. As these pretences are universal, no-one is deceived; they are trouble thrown away.

From these contradictions arises a result which we constantly feel in our own persons. Driven in opposite directions by nature and by custom, and forced to yield somewhat to both, we take a half-way road that leads us to neither goal. Thus, tossed about and drifting all our lives, we end our days unable to make for ourselves a consistent character or to be of any use either to ourselves or to others.

There remains, then, only private education, or that of nature. But of what use, you will say, will a man be to others who is educated only for himself? Yet it may be that, if we could but reduce our two proposed aims to one, we should, by taking away contradictory motives, remove a great obstacle to happiness. To judge of this possibility, we must look at our pupil at the end of his

[1] To show his practical attitude on this matter, a letter to a parent is added (see *d* on p. 71).

education; we must have observed his tendencies, have traced his progress, and followed it stage by stage; in a word, we must have learned to know Nature's Man. I flatter myself that the reader will have made some advance in this direction when he has finished this treatise.

Let us now consider what we have to do in order to form this rare being. Doubtless it is a serious undertaking; for we have to prevent *anything* from being done. When it is only the wind which is against us, we can tack; but, when the current is likewise strong, if we would not lose ground, we are obliged to drop anchor. Take care, young pilot, that your cable does not veer or your anchor drag, and your ship drive before you are aware.

In the social order, where all the places are marked out, everyone must be educated for his own. If an individual leaves the position for which he has been trained, he is unfit for any other. Education is useful only if fortune favours parents' intentions; in every other case it is harmful, be it only by reason of the prejudices which it has instilled. In Egypt, where the son was obliged to follow his father's occupation, education had at least an assured end; but among us, where classes only are permanent and their members are constantly changing, a father is not sure whether, in bringing up his child to his own profession, he may not be doing him an injury.

In the natural order all men are equal, manhood is their common vocation; and anyone who is well trained for this vocation can not fulfil amiss any other which is related to it. It matters little to me whether my pupil be designed for the army, the church, or the bar. Nature has destined us to live as men. To live is the profession I would teach him. When I have done with him, it is true, he will be neither a lawyer, a soldier, nor a divine. He will first be a man; anything else that a man ought to be he will become as occasion arises as soon as any other. Fortune may remove him from rank to rank as she pleases, he will always be in his place. *Occupavi te, fortuna, atque cepi: omnesque aditus tuos interclusi, ut ad me aspirare non posses.*

The lot of man is our true study. He that is best able to bear its goods and ills is, I hold, the most truly educated; true education lies less in knowing than in doing. We begin to learn when we begin to live; education commences with life, the nurse is the first teacher. . . .

We must, therefore, take a wide view and consider our pupil as a man, not as some particular kind of man; as a man, exposed to all the accidents of a man's life. If men were born inseparably attached to the soil of one country, if one season lasted the whole year, if no-one could be dislodged from his present station, then existing modes of education would, in some respects, be sound; a child would be brought up for his station, he would never leave it and he would never be exposed to the difficulties of any other. But when we consider the instability of human affairs, the restless and changeful spirit of the age, which reverses everything with each new generation; can we conceive any method of education more absurd than that of bringing up a child as if he would never leave his nursery and would be perpetually surrounded by attendants? If the helpless creature puts a foot on the ground or comes down one step of the stairs, his doom is sealed! We are not teaching him to bear pain, we are preparing him to feel it more acutely.

We think only of preserving his life and limb. It is not enough; he ought to be taught how to preserve them himself when he is grown up; to endure the shocks of fortune, to bear riches or poverty, and to live, if occasion require, amid the snows of Iceland or on the burning rocks of Malta. You may take what precautions you will to preserve his life, yet he is bound to die; and even if his death is not the result of your precautions, in any case they will have done him harm. It is of less moment to preserve him from death than to teach him how to live. To live is not merely to breathe; it is to act, to make a proper use of our organs, our senses, our faculties, and all parts of our being which contribute to our consciousness of life. He has not had most life who has lived most years, but he who has felt life the most. A man may be buried a hundred years old and have died in his cradle. Such an one would have gained by dying in youth if he had *lived* till then.

Our wisdom consists of servile prejudices; our customs are nothing but subjection, restriction, constraint. Civilized man is born, lives, dies in slavery : at his birth he is bound in swaddling clothes, at his death nailed in his coffin; and, all the time he has worn the image of man, he has been held no less fast by our institutions.

b. Extract from the Treatise on the Government of Poland.

(Chapter IV., Education.)

Education—this is the essential point. It is education which must shape their minds in the national mould and which must direct their tastes and their opinions, till they are patriotic by inclination—by instinct—by necessity. A child should see his **father-land** when he first opens his eyes, and till death he should see nought else. The true republican sucks in with his mother's milk the love of his country, that is of law and liberty. This love makes up his life; he only sees his fatherland, and only lives for his fatherland; alone, he is nothing; his country lost, he lives no more; if not dead, he is worse.

National education belongs only to the free; they alone live a national life, they alone are truly bound by law. A Frenchman, an Englishman, a Spaniard, an Italian, and a Russian are almost alike; they leave college ready fashioned for a life of licence—and licence spells slavery. At twenty a Pole should be nothing else; he should be a Pole. When he learns to read, he should read of his country; at ten he should know all its products, at twelve he should know all its provinces, roads and towns, at fifteen all its history, at sixteen all its laws; there should not be in all Poland a noble deed or a famous man that he does not know and love, or that he could not describe on the spot. You can see that I would not tolerate the usual course of study directed by priests and by foreigners. Subjects, order and method must be controlled by law. Teachers should all be Poles, if possible married men, and all marked out by character, trustworthiness, good sense and ability. They should all be destined for posts, not more important nor more honourable—for that is impossible—but less exhausting and more distinguished, at the end of a certain number of years spent in teaching. Always be careful not to make teaching a trade. No public man in Poland should have any permanent occupation but that of a citizen. All the posts he fills, especially the more important, such as that of a teacher, should be considered simply as probationary steps by which he may mount to a higher rung of the ladder after he has shown his capacities. I urge the Poles to pay great attention to this principle, on which I shall frequently insist; for I believe it to be a spring which sets in action a great motive power in the State. Later on, I shall try to show how I believe it can be made invariably effective.

I do not approve of the distinction between "colleges" and "academies," which means that the wealthy nobles and the poorer nobles are educated separately and on a different plan. As they are all equal by the terms of the constitution, they should all be educated together, and in a similar manner. If public education cannot be made entirely free of charge, the fee should at least be such as the poorer members can afford. Could not a number of free places be established in every college at the expense of the State, such as are called in France "bursaries"? Such places, given to the sons of poor gentlemen who had done good service to the State, not as charity, but as a reward for their fathers' services, would come to be considered as a mark of honour, and might thus produce a twofold advantage which should not be overlooked. To achieve this object, it would be necessary that the awards should not be arbitrary, but should be made after a process of enquiry which will be described below. The holders would be called children of the State, and distinguished by some badge of honour which would give them precedence over other children of their age, not excepting those of high rank.

A gymnasium for physical exercise should be established in every college. This neglected side of education is, I hold, its most important branch, not only as the basis of a sound and healthy physique, but still more as a training of character. The latter aim is at present either wholly neglected or based on a mass of useless pedantic precepts which are a mere waste of breath. I can never repeat too often that true education must be negative. Prevent the growth of vices and you will have done enough for virtue. The means are perfectly easy in a good system of state education. You have only to abandon those wearisome studies, which children do not understand, and which they hate simply because they oblige them to sit still, and to train them by means of bodily exercises, which they enjoy, because they satisfy the demand of the growing body for movement. The very fact that they enjoy them will make them beneficial outside the purely physical sphere.

They should not be allowed to play separately according to their fancy, but all together and in public, so that they always have a common aim involving co-operation and competition. Parents who prefer a private education and wish to bring up their children under their own eyes should nevertheless send them to join in these exercises. Their lessons may be private and individual, but their games should always be public and common; for the function of games is not merely to occupy children, and to give them a strong physique or free and agile movements, but to accustom them early to discipline, equality, fraternity, and co-operation, to live in the gaze of their fellow-citizens and to desire public approval. To achieve this purpose, the prizes and rewards of successful competitors should not be awarded at the sole discretion of the physical instructor or of the head master, but by the verdict of the spectators as shown by their applause. It may be assumed that such estimates will always be fair, especially if care be taken to make these games attractive to the public by conducting them with a certain amount of ceremony as is customary in the case of public exhibitions. Thus it may be granted that all respectable and patriotic persons will regard it as a duty and a pleasure to assist in them. . . .

Whatever system of state education is adopted, into the details of which I shall not enter, it is desirable to establish a committee of officials of the highest rank who shall have the supreme control and shall appoint, dismiss, and change at will all principals and heads of colleges (who shall themselves be, as I have stated, candidates for the higher offices) as well as all physical instructors, who should be encouraged to a careful and zealous performance of their duties by the hope of promotion to higher posts, which will or will not be allotted to them according to the manner in which they have carried out their existing duties. As it is on these institutions that the hope of the state, the reputation and destiny of the nation depends, I attach to them, I admit, an importance which I am very surprised to find is not accorded them in any other quarter. I pity mankind when I see so many ideas which strike me as sound and useful, so far from being carried into effect, though perfectly easy of execution!

This is only a brief outline, but it is enough for the readers whom I am addressing. These ill-arranged notes give a distant view of those paths—unknown to modern peoples—by which ancient states led their citizens to a vigour of spirit, a patriotic zeal, a regard for the bed-rock of a man's character irrespective of its adventitious embellishments, which to-day are unknown. The leaven is ready in the hearts of men, awaiting suitable institutions to make it ferment. Direct the education, habits, customs and characters of the Poles in this spirit, and you will stir this leaven, which has not been moved by degenerate maxims, conventional institutions, and a selfish philosophy which preaches and kills. The nation will date its second birth from the crisis out of which it is now passing. . . .

c. Letter to Dr. Tronchin (November 27, 1758).

In regard to the circles, I admit their faults, and do not doubt them : such is the fate of human institutions ; but I believe that with the abolition of the circles worse evils will ensue. You make a very wise distinction between the Greek republics and our own in regard to public education ; but this does not prevent such education having its place in our city and having it from the mere force of our conditions, whether we wish it or no. Consider what a difference there is between our artisans and those of other countries. A Geneva watchmaker is presentable anywhere ; a Paris watchmaker can only talk about watches. The education of a workman in his craft trains his hands and no more. Yet there remains the citizen to be considered. For good or ill the heart and head are being formed ; there is always time for this training ; and it is this to which education ought to look. On this subject I have the advantage over you in the concrete case which you have over me as regards general principles ; my own position is that of an artisan ; it is the station into which I was born, in which I ought to have lived, and which I abandoned only to my own loss. I received this public education, not indeed in the shape of formal instruction, but of traditions and maxims, which, handed on from generation to generation, gave to my early boyhood the knowledge which it required and the feelings which it needed. At twelve I was a Roman ; at twenty I had scoured the world and was no better than a tramp. Times, I know, have changed; but it is unfair to make the artisans the scapegoats of the general degeneracy : it is well known that it was not among them that it began. The rich are always corrupted first; the poor follow; the middle classes are the last affected. Among us the middle classes are represented by watchmakers.

It is bad if the children are left to their own devices. But why are they ? It is not the fault of the circles; on the contrary, it is there that they ought to be brought up, the girls by the mothers, the boys by the fathers. That is precisely the middle course which suits us, half-way between the public education of a Greek republic and the private education of a monarchical state, in which all the subjects must remain isolated and have nothing in common save obedience.

The exercises of which I approve must not be confounded with those of an ancient gymnasium. The latter constituted a regular occupation, almost a trade; ours should be only a relaxation, a holiday; and it was only in that sense that I proposed them. Since amusements are necessary, these are the kind which should be presented to us. In my time it was often remarked in Geneva that the most capable workmen were those who most distinguished themselves in these kind of exercises which were then in vogue among us : this is a proof that the two occupations did not hinder one another but, on the contrary, were a mutual help. The time which the citizens gave to them left less time for vicious pleasures and maintained a higher standard of character.

d. Letter to the Countess of Boufflers.

. . . I see in truth great disadvantages in sending young people to Universities; but I see too that circumstances may make it a more serious disadvantage not to send them; and it is not always a question of choosing the greater of two goods, but the less of two evils. Besides, once the necessity of such a course is granted, I agree with you that there is less danger in Holland than anywhere else.

e. From the *Émile* (further on in Book I.).

[This passage is taken from the part where Rousseau is stating the conditions for which he chooses his imaginary pupil.]

The poor have no need of education; that of their station is forced upon them and they could make no use of any other. On the other hand, the education which the rich receive from their station is the least adapted either to their own good or to the good of society. Besides, natural education ought to qualify a man for all conditions of life: now it is certainly less reasonable to educate the poor to be rich than the rich to be poor; for, in proportion to the number of both, there are fewer poor persons who become rich than there are rich persons who become poor. Our pupil therefore shall be rich: thus we are at least sure of forming one man the more; the poor child may become a man for himself.

[See also the concluding portion of the *Émile*, pp. 257-262, for the ultimate education of *Émile* for citizenship.]

3. EDUCATION AND THE FAMILY.

Émile (Book I.   Much condensed.)

[After the passage on p. 64, Rousseau goes on to attack the swaddling of children, which he traces to the desire of nurses to avoid trouble; he then attacks the custom of giving children to nurses.]

Do these polished mothers who, escaped from their children, indulge themselves gaily in the amusements of the town know the treatment which their innocent babes in their swathings are enduring in the country? . . .

Not content with having ceased to suckle their children, women have acquired a reluctance to their production; indeed the one is a natural consequence of the other. This practice, added to other causes of depopulation, forebodes the approaching fate of Europe. The sciences, arts, philosophy, and manners, to which Europe has given rise, will not save it from being reduced ere long to a desert. It will be peopled only by wild beasts; nor will it have greatly changed its inhabitants.

I have frequently observed the little artifices of some newly-married women who affect to be desirous of nursing their own children. They know very well how to get themselves urged to give up the point. A husband who would dare to consent that his wife should nurse her child would be considered an abandoned wretch.

Ought the question to be considered only from the physical side? Has a child less need of a mother's tenderness than of her breast? Other women, nay brutes, can give it the milk which she refuses; but the tenderness of a mother cannot be supplied. She who suckles the child of another instead of her own must be a bad mother; how then can she make a good nurse? She may become so in time, but slowly, as habit takes the place of nature; meanwhile the neglected child will have a hundred opportunities to perish before his nurse has acquired a mother's love for him.

Even if this advantage is secured, it involves an inconvenience which is enough to deter a woman of feeling from committing her children to the care of others; she is sharing her mother's rights, or rather abandoning them to another; she sees her child love another woman as well or better than herself; she feels that the affection which it retains for its natural parent is a matter of favour, while that which it feels for its adopted parent is a duty; for should not a child's love go where it finds a mother's care?

Would you have everyone return to his first duties, begin with mothers; you will be astonished at the changes which you will effect. This is the source from which degeneracy has gradually spread till the whole moral order is broken; natural feeling is extinguished in our hearts; our homes have become less cheerful; the touching sight of growing children no longer attaches the husband nor attracts the eyes of strangers; the mother is less respected whose children are not about her; families are no longer places of residence; habit no longer enforces the ties of blood; there are no fathers nor mothers, children, brothers nor sisters; they hardly know—how should they love?—each other. Each cares for no-one but himself; and when home affords only a melancholy solitude, it is natural for us to seek diversion elsewhere.

Should mothers again condescend to nurse their children, manners would be reformed of themselves; the sentiments of nature would revive in our hearts; the state would be repeopled—this first point would by itself embrace everything. The charms of family life are the best antidote against corruption of manners. The shouts of children, which now seem troublesome, become attractive; they make the father and mother more necessary and more dear to one another; they bind the marriage tie more fast. When a family is gay and lively, household cares are a woman's dearest occupation and a husband's most agreeable amusement. Hence, from the correction of this one abuse, will presently result a general reform; nature will soon reassert her rights everywhere. Let wives once more become mothers, and men will soon once more become fathers and husbands.

Where there is no mother, there can be no child. Their obligations are reciprocal, and, if they are neglected on one side, they will hardly be fulfilled on the other. The child should love his mother before he knows it to be his duty. If the voice of blood be not strengthened by care and habit, it will be silenced in infancy and the heart will die before it is born. Such are our first steps away from nature.

As his mother is his only true nurse, so is his father his only true tutor. He will be better educated by a judicious father, though of limited ability, than by the ablest master in the world; for zeal will better supply the place of abilities than abilities compensate for want of zeal.

But, it will be said, business, occupations, duties— duties! doubtless those of the father are of the least importance! We need not be surprised that the man whose wife disdains to nourish the fruit of their union should similarly disdain to educate it. There is no picture in the world more delightful than that of a family; but the lack of a single feature spoils the whole. If the mother is too weak to be a nurse, the father is too busy to be a tutor. Their children, sent from home and dispersed in boarding-schools, convents, and colleges, will carry their family affection elsewhere, or rather will form the habit of being attached to nothing. Brothers and sisters hardly know each other. When they are all gathered together on some ceremonial occasion, they will behave to each other as politely as to strangers. When intimacy between relations no longer subsists, when family affection no longer contributes to the pleasures of life, then men have recourse to the corruption of manners to supply the lack. Where is the man so blind as not to see the connexion?

A father in begetting and providing for his children has discharged but the third part of his obligations. He owes a being to his species, a social being to society, and a citizen to the state. Every man who is able to pay this triple debt and refuses is culpable in this respect; perhaps he is more culpable when he pays it by halves.

IV

SELECTIONS FROM "ÉMILE," BOOK I. (ON THE EDUCATION OF CHILDREN UNDER FIVE)

[As much of this book deals with the more physical side of education, and some of it represents views taken from others, no attempt has been made to give it in full.]

1. PHYSICAL TRAINING.

THE body should be vigorous, in order to obey the mind, just as a good servant should be robust. Intemperance inflames the passions, and in time wears away the body : fastings and mortifications produce the same effect in a different manner. The feebler the body, the more it rules : the stronger, the more it obeys. The sensual passions all lodge in effeminate bodies.

An enfeebled body enervates the mind. Hence the influence of medicine, an art more destructive to mankind than all the evils which it pretends to cure. I know not, for my part, of what malady we are cured by physicians, but I know many fatal maladies which they inflict on us—cowardice, pusillanimity, credulity, and fear of death. If they cure the body of pain, they rob the soul of fortitude.

[A long attack on physicians and valetudinarianism follows.]

The only useful part of medicine is hygiene, and hygiene is rather a virtue than a science. Temperance and work are the two best physicians in the world. Work whets the appetite, and temperance prevents its abuse. . . . I shall not detain the reader while I prove the utility of manual labour and of bodily exercise in strengthening the constitution and in preserving health : it is a point which no one disputes : instances of longevity are almost all found among persons who have been accustomed to exercise and who have undergone the greatest labour and fatigue.

[A long passage on the choice of a nurse follows. The child is to be taken into the country.]

Men were not made to be massed together in shoals, but to spread over the earth which they must till. The more they gather together, the more they corrupt one another. Infirmity of body and depravity of mind are the inevitable effect of too close a concourse. Man is of all animals the least adapted to live in herds. Men who should gather into flocks like sheep would all quickly perish. The breath of man is destructive to his fellows; this is true in a literal no less than in a figurative sense. Cities are the graves of mankind. At the end of a few generations, their inhabitants perish or degenerate ; they require to be renewed, and it is always the country which regenerates the stock. Send your children therefore to renew their strength in the country, and to recover in the open fields that vigour which is lost in the unwholesome air of popular cities.

[Bathing and the absence of swaddling-clothes are then discussed.]

2. Training of the Senses.

We are born with a capacity for acquiring knowledge, but without actual knowledge. The soul, confined in imperfect and undeveloped organs, has no sense even of its own existence. The movements and cries of a new-born infant are purely mechanical effects, void of knowledge and of will.

Let us suppose that a child possessed at birth the strength and stature of a grown man, that it came into being armed at all points, like Pallas issuing from the head of Jupiter. This child-man would be a perfect idiot, an automaton, an immovable and almost insensible statue. He would see nothing, understand nothing, recognize no one; nay, he could not even turn his eyes towards the object which he required to see. He would perceive nothing as external to him; he would not even locate his sensations in their respective organs. Colours would not be localized in the eye, sounds in the ear, nor contiguous bodies on the skin—he would not know that he possessed a body. The feeling of touch would appear to be situate in the brain; all his sensations would be centralized in a single point: he would exist only in the common sensorium. He would have but one idea, that of self, in which all his feelings would be absorbed; and this idea, or rather sensation, would constitute the only difference between such a being and an ordinary child.

Nor would the being who had thus been formed in a moment be able to stand on his feet: he would be a long time in learning how to keep his balance; perhaps he would not even attempt it, and you would see this tall, strong, robust animal fixed in one place like a stone, or crawling and tumbling like a puppy.

He would feel the uneasiness occasioned by his wants,

but he would not understand them or know any means of satisfying them. There is no immediate communication between the muscles of the stomach and those of the legs and arms such as would cause him, even if he were surrounded with food, to take a single step to approach it or to reach out his hand to lay hold of it. . . .

We now know, or are in a position to know, the starting-point from which we all set out towards the ordinary degree of understanding; but who knows the other extremity of the line? Everyone makes more or less progress according to his character, his tastes, his necessities, his talents, his zeal, and the opportunities which are afforded him. I know of no philosopher who has been rash enough to prescribe a limit which a man cannot pass. We do not know what Nature allows us to become; no-one has measured the distance between one man and another. Where is the mind so base as never to have been elevated by this reflexion? Who has not sometimes said in his pride, "How many men have I not already surpassed! How many may not I yet overtake? Why should my equal go further than myself?"

Again I repeat, the education of man begins at birth; before he can speak, before he can understand, he is already learning. Experience anticipates lessons; the moment he recognizes his nurse, he has already learned much. Trace the progress of the most ignorant of mortals from birth to the present moment, and you will be astonished at the knowledge which he has acquired. If we divide all human knowledge into two parts, the one that which is common to mankind and the other that which is peculiar to the learned, the latter will appear insignificant in comparison with the former. . . .

The first sensations of children are purely affective;

they perceive nothing but pleasure and pain. Being unable to walk or grip, they take a considerable time in building up those representative sensations which reveal objects as having an external existence. Nevertheless, while objects have still to assume extension, to retreat as it were from the eye, and to assume forms and dimensions, the recurrence of affective sensations begins to subjugate children to the empire of habit. Their eyes are constantly turned towards the light, and, if it come from one side, they imperceptibly take that direction; so that care should always be taken to place them facing the light, lest they contract a squint or become accustomed to look sideways. They should also be early accustomed to darkness, otherwise they will be apt to cry when they find themselves in the dark.

If the allowance of sleep and food is too carefully regulated, they become necessary at stated intervals, and after a time a craving arises, not from physical necessity, but from habit, or rather habit adds a new need to those of nature: this must by all means be prevented.

The only habit which a child should be allowed to form is that of forming none; he should not be carried in one arm more than the other; he should not be accustomed to hold out his right hand oftener than his left, or to use one more than the other; he should not want to eat, to sleep, or to do anything, at stated hours; he should not mind being left alone, whether by day or night. Prepare him early for the enjoyment of liberty and the exercise of his powers; leave his body its natural habits; enable him always to be master of himself and, as soon as he acquires a will, always to carry out its dictates.

As soon as a child begins to distinguish objects, a careful choice should be made of those which are presented to him.   Every new object is naturally interesting to a child.   His weakness makes him afraid of everything which he does not recognize : accustom him to see new objects without being affected by them and you destroy this timidity.   Children who are brought up in neat houses, where cobwebs are carefully swept away, are always afraid of spiders, and often continue to fear them when they grow up; but I never knew a peasant, man or woman, afraid of a spider.

Why, then, should not the education of a child begin before it can speak or understand, since even the choice of the objects which are presented to its gaze is enough to make it either timid or courageous ?   I would have them accustomed to seeing new objects—ugly, repulsive, and uncommon animals—but by degrees and at a distance, till they grow used to them, and, seeing others handle them, venture to do so themselves.

[He then quotes from the *Iliad* the action of Hector when his child was afraid of the plume on his helmet, and explains how he would accustom Émile to the sound of firearms.]

During infancy, when memory and imagination are still inactive, a child attends only to those sensations which actually affect his senses with pain or pleasure. His sensations are the raw material of his ideas; by supplying sensations in the right order we therefore prepare his memory to present them in the same order to his understanding : but, as he is at present capable of attending only to sensations, it is enough for a time to show him clearly the connection between these sensations and the objects which excite them.   He wants to touch and handle everything which he sees : do not check this restlessness; it is a necessary apprenticeship to learning. It is thus that he must learn to distinguish heat and cold, hardness and softness, weight and lightness, and to judge of size, shape, and other sensible qualities. These lessons he learns by looking, touching, and listening, but above all by comparing sight with touch and by estimating with the eye the sensations which would be given to the fingers.

It is by movement that we discover the existence of external objects, and by our own movements that we acquire the idea of extension. It is because a child has no such idea that he stretches out his hand in the same way to lay hold of an object that is within reach and another which is a hundred yards distant. . . . Take care therefore if you wish him to judge distance to change his position frequently, and to carry him from place to place in such a way as to make him realize the change of position. When once he begins to realize the difference, your method must be changed; you must now carry him only where you please, not where he pleases: for when he is no longer deceived by his senses, the efforts of which I have been speaking change their motive.

3. Moral Training.

As man, in the first stage of life, is a miserable helpless being, his first mode of expression consists of tears and complaints. An infant feels his wants but cannot satisfy them, so he implores the assistance of those about him by his cries. . . . Thus from the tears of children, which we are apt to think so little worthy of attention, arises the first relation of man to his surroundings: here is forged the first link of that chain which forms the bond of society.

When a child cries, he is uneasy; he has some want

which he cannot satisfy; we look, we examine what it is, find it out, and relieve it. If we cannot find it out or relieve it, his tears continue to flow; we are disturbed; we try to quiet him with soothing words; we rock him or try to sing him to sleep; if this does not succeed, we grow impatient and threaten him; sometimes a brutal nurse will beat him.

[He gives an instance.]

This example alone would have convinced me, if I could ever have doubted it, that there is an innate sense of right and wrong implanted in the human heart. I am sure that, if a burning coal had fallen by accident on the child's hand, it would have been less agitated than by this slight blow given with a manifest intention to hurt it. This disposition in children to passion and excessive anger needs careful treatment. . . . As long as children are crossed only by the resistance of things and not by persons, they will never grow fractious or passionate and their health will be better. This is one reason why the children of common people, being more free and independent, are generally less weak and delicate than the more carefully educated children who are being perpetually crossed. It must, however, be remembered that it is a very different thing to humour a child and to avoid crossing him.

The first tears of young children are requests; if we are not careful, they will soon become commands; they begin by begging our help, they end by making us their slaves. Thus, from their very weakness, whence at first arises the sense of their dependence, there soon follows the notion of domineering and command. This idea, being excited less by their own wants than by our care, is the first evidence of moral effects of which the immediate cause is not due to nature. . . . All vice takes its rise from weakness; an infant is vicious only because he is weak; give him power and you make him good. An all-powerful Being could never do ill. . . .

Reason alone teaches us to know good and evil. Conscience, which makes us love good and hate evil, though it is independent of reason, cannot develop apart from it. Before the age of reason, we do good and evil without knowing it; there is no morality in our own actions, though a moral element is sometimes found in our feelings concerning the conduct of others towards us. A child will disturb everything he sees, will break everything he approaches, will seize a bird as he would a stone, and will kill it without knowing what he is doing. Why? A philosopher will immediately attribute such conduct to the vices which are inherent in our nature, to the pride, tyranny, selfishness, and wickedness of man: the sense of weakness, he will add, makes the child eager to perform acts of violence in order to prove his power. But look at the infirm and decayed old man, whom the cycle of human life has brought back to the weakness of childhood: he is quiet and peaceable, he wishes that everything around him should be the same. . . . Where are we to look for the explanation, unless in their different physical constitutions? The active principle, which both share, is developing in the child and contracting in the old man. The one is growing, the other decaying; the one is on the threshold of life, the other of death. Failing energy concentrates in the case of the old; in the child it overflows and spreads outward; he seems to have enough life to animate everything around him. Whether he makes or mars matters not, provided he causes a change, and every change is an action. If he seems more ready to destroy, it is not from malice, but because construction is slow while destruction is rapid; the latter agrees better with his natural impetuosity.

When the Creator implanted this active principle in children, He took care to make it harmless by giving them little strength for its indulgence. But once they come to regard other people as instruments which they can put in action, they will use them in the pursuit of their inclinations to make up for their own weakness. That is how they become troublesome, tyrannical, imperious, mischievous, and intractable. . . . The desire of command does not die out with the needs which gave it birth; the tyrannical spirit flatters their self-esteem and is strengthed by habit: primitive needs are succeeded by fanciful needs, and the prejudices of artificial notions first take root.

This principle once recognized, we see clearly the point at which we leave the path of nature: let us now consider what must be done to keep to it. So far from having superfluous powers, children at first have hardly enough for all Nature's demands; let them enjoy those which she has given them and which they cannot abuse. This is my first maxim. We should help them by making up for all their deficiences of mind or body, in every case of physical necessity. This is the second maxim. Help should be confined to real needs, no concession should be made to caprice or unreasonable desires; they will never be troubled by caprice unless we have fostered its growth, for it is no part of their original nature. That is the third. . . .

The purpose of these rules is to give children more real liberty and less right to command, to let them do more for themselves and require less of others. Thus they will be early accustomed to limit their desires by their capacities and will not feel the lack of anything which is beyond the power to secure. Here we have a new and important reason for leaving their body and limbs at full liberty.

[He then reverts to the treatment of crying.]

[The book ends with a section on teaching children to talk, the chief points of which are as follows: (1) Articulate words are useless when addressed to very young children; (2) we should not trouble to correct child-syntax; (3) we are in too great a hurry to teach them to speak; (4) we should make them speak clearly by not taking care to listen to them if they do not; (5) inexpressive speech is largely due to the amount which they have to say by heart; (6) their vocabulary should not outrun their understanding.]

V

" ÉMILE," BOOK II. (ON EDUCATION FROM FIVE TO TWELVE)

[This book has been reduced to about one-third of the original text, but it is hoped that the slight synopses of the parts omitted give a continuous sense.]

1. MORAL TRAINING.

a. Hardihood.

WHEN a child begins to talk, he cries less. This change is natural; one language is substituted for the other. . . . If a child is delicate and sensitive and naturally apt to cry for no reason, I would soon dry up the source of his tears by rendering them fruitless. So long as he cries I do not go near him, but I run to him immediately he stops. His manner of calling me will soon be to keep quiet or at most to utter a single cry.

If he falls, bumps his forehead, makes his nose bleed, or cuts his fingers, instead of running to him with an air of alarm, I shall remain quite still, at least for a short time. The mischief is done and he must bear it; all my anxiety would only serve to frighten him the more and to increase his sensitiveness. In fact it is less the pain than the fright which affects children when they are hurt. . . . If he sees me make light of it, he will soon

87

make light of it himself. . . . It is at this age that children learn their first lessons in courage; and, not being alarmed by slight pains, learn by degrees to bear greater.

So far from being anxious to prevent Émile hurting himself, I should be very sorry if it did not sometimes happen, and if he grew up without feeling pain. The first lesson we ought to learn, the most important thing for us to know, is how to suffer. It seems as if children were formed small and feeble only to learn this important lesson without danger. . . . I do not know any instance of a child, when left at liberty, having killed or maimed or severely injured himself. . . . Instead of keeping him stifling in the close air of his nursery, he should be taken out every day into the open fields. There he might run and play about; and, if he tumbles a hundred times a day, so much the better; he will learn more quickly how to get up again. The pleasures of liberty will repay him for many falls. . . .

b. The Child to be considered as a Child.

Though the maximum term of human life is fairly determinate, and it is easy to calculate the average expectancy of life at any age, yet nothing is more uncertain than the duration of individual lives; very few reach the maximum. Life is most precarious in early years; the shorter the time we have lived, the smaller are our chances of living. Of all the children that are born, half at most reach adolescence, and it is probable that your pupil will not reach manhood. What can we think then of that barbarous education which sacrifices the present to an uncertain future, which lays a child under every kind of restraint and makes his early life miserable, to prepare him for a pretended happiness which there is every reason to believe he may never live to enjoy ?   Even if we supposed the object to be reasonable, how could we avoid indignation at the sight of unhappy innocents subjected to a yoke of intolerable rigour, condemned like galley-slaves to continual labour, unless we were assured that such restrictions would some day be of service to them ? The age of gaiety is spent amid tears, punishments, threats, and slavery. . . . Man ! be humane ! It is your first duty to all ages, to all conditions, to every creature with which man has to deal.   What wisdom can there be without humanity ?   Love childhood ; look kindly on its play, its pleasures, its lovable instincts. . .

You will perhaps reply, " This is the time to correct the evil tendencies of human nature.   It is in childhood, when our pains are least felt, that they should be multiplied, to diminish their number when we arrive at years of discretion."   But who has told you that such an arrangement is in your power ?   Or that all the fine instruction with which you load the weak mind of a child will not one day be more pernicious than useful to him ? . . .   As mankind has its place in the world, so has childhood its place in human life ; we should consider the man in the man and the child in the child. To assign to each his separate place and keep him in it, to regulate human passions by human nature, is all that we can do for his well-being.   The rest depends on external circumstances which are not under our control. . . .

c. Equilibrium of Desires and Capacities.

In what consists human wisdom or the road to true happiness ?   Not exactly in diminishing our desires ; for, if these were less than our capacities, part of our faculties would remain idle, and we should enjoy but half our being. Nor again in extending our faculties; for if our desires were extended at the same time in a greater proportion, we should only become more miserable. (It must consist therefore in lessening the disproportion between our capacities and our desires, in reducing our inclinations and our powers to a perfect equilibrium.) It is thus only that all our faculties can be employed, that the mind can nevertheless preserve its tranquillity, and that the whole man can feel a perfect adjustment.

It is thus that Nature, which always acts for the best, constitutes us at birth. At first she gives us only such desires as are necessary for our preservation and the faculties necessary to satisfy them. All the rest she keeps, as it were, in reserve in the storehouse of the soul, to develop as they are needed. It is only in this primitive state that there is equilibrium between desires and capacities and that man is not unhappy. As soon as his potentialities are raised to action, Imagination, the most active of them all, awakes and outstrips the others. It is Imagination which extends the horizon of our possibilities, both for good and ill; this is the power which excites and nourishes our desires with the hope of satisfying them. But the object, which at first appears to be within our grasp, flies more quickly than we can pursue; or, when we think we have reached it, there is a transformation and it reappears far ahead. We see no more the distance which we have run, and count it as nothing; that which remains spreads out before our gaze and never ceases to grow; our efforts bring us no nearer the goal; the more we gain upon enjoyment, the more happiness outdistances us.

On the other hand, the nearer man remains to his

natural condition, the less is the difference between his desires and his capacities, and the nearer he is to happiness. Man is never less miserable than when he appears utterly destitute; misery does not consist in the absence of possessions, but in the need which we feel of them.

The real world has its limits, the imaginary world is infinite: as we cannot enlarge the one, let us contract the other; for it is their difference only that gives birth to all those troubles that make us unhappy. If we except health, strength, and a good conscience, all the blessings of life are the creation of our thoughts. Except bodily pain and the pangs of conscience, all our evils are imaginary. "A trite principle," it may be said. I confess it, but the practical application of it is not common; and it is the practice only which we are now considering.

[The principle is illustrated by a variety of cases.]

d. No Dependence on Men.

A man can only do as he pleases when he needs not to use the arms of another for his purpose. Hence it follows that the greatest of all blessings is not authority but liberty. The man who is really free only desires what he can perform; he can then perform all that he desires. This is my fundamental maxim. It needs only to be applied to children and all the rules of education will flow from it. . . .

If man is strong and a child weak, it is not because the man has more absolute strength than the child, but because the man can supply his own needs and the child can not. . . . This is the reason for the weakness of children; Nature has provided for it by the attachment of parents to their offspring. This attachment is liable

to excess, to defect, or to abuse. Parents who live in
a civilized state introduce their children to it too young.
By increasing their wants, instead of relieving, they
augment their weakness. They augment it still further
by adding to the demands of Nature, by subjecting to
the will of the parent the little strength that a child
has to execute his own, and by converting into servility
on one side or on the other the reciprocal dependence
which weakness imposes on the child and attachment on
the parent.

A wise man can keep his place : a child does not know
his place and cannot therefore keep it. There are a
thousand avenues through which he may escape from
it : it is the duty of his educators to prevent him, and it
is no easy task. He should be treated neither as an
animal nor as a man, but as a child ; he should be made
to feel his weakness, but not to suffer by it ; he should
be dependent but not obedient ; he should ask but not
command. He is subject to others only by reason of
his needs, because others know better than himself what
is good for him and what does or does not conduce to
his preservation. No-one, not even his father, has a right
to lay any needless commands on a child. . . .

There are two kinds of dependence : the first on things,
which is that of Nature ; the second on men, which is the
effect of society. The former, being non-moral, does not
destroy liberty nor give rise to vices : the latter, being
unnatural, produces a rich crop : the relation of master
and slave depraves both. . . . Keep your child dependent
only on things ; you will then be following the order of
nature in the progress of his education. Oppose to his
indiscreet desires only physical obstacles, or the punishments which arise out of the actions themselves. These
he will remember on a future occasion ; you need not

forbid him to do ill, it is enough to prevent him. Experience or inability should take the place of law. Give him nothing because he desires it, but because he needs it. Let him not be conscious of obedience when he acts for himself nor of command when you act for him. Let him recognize a freedom of choice equally in his own actions and in yours. Assist him, when he needs assistance, just so much as will make him free but not imperious, he will then receive your assistance with a kind of humiliation and will long for the moment when he can do without it and can have the honour of serving himself.

To strengthen the body and assist it in its growth, Nature employs various means which should never be thwarted. We should never oblige a child to stand still when he wishes to walk, nor to walk when he wishes to stand still. If the liberty of children is not spoiled by our own mistakes, they will never wish for anything useless. Let them jump, run about, and make what noise they please. All their movements express the needs of a constitution which is striving to gain strength. But we ought to distrust every desire which they cannot satisfy for themselves, and for which they have to ask our help. We must carefully distinguish the true physical need from those capricious needs which now begin to appear, and from those which arise merely from the superfluity of vital energy which was discussed above. . . .

When a request is prompted by a real need, you ought to recognize the fact and to comply at once; but to give way to his tears is to encourage them, to teach him to doubt your good-will and to think that you are influenced more by importunity than by benevolence. If he does not think you good, he will soon become bad; if he thinks you weak, he will soon grow obstinate. You should immediately grant what you do not intend to refuse. Do not refuse often, but never revoke a refusal.

Above all, beware of teaching your child the empty forms of politeness, which he will treat as magic syllables, capable of subjecting everything about him to his pleasure. . . . You can see immediately that in his mouth "If you please" means "I please," and that "I beg" means "I order" . . . .

Do you know the surest way to make your child miserable? To accustom him to get everything he wants! Since his desires are ever increasing with the power of gratifying them, sooner or later he will ask the impossible; you will be obliged unwillingly to refuse; and this unprecedented refusal will give him even more pain than the want of the expected gratification. . . . I have known children who have been thus brought up ask their nurse to pull down the house, cry for the weather-cock on the steeple, demand that a regiment should be stopped on the march that they might listen to the drum, pierce the air with their cries, and refuse to listen to anyone when their requests were not immediately granted. . . .

The words "command" and "obey" should be banished from his vocabulary, still more "duty" and "obligation": "compulsion," "necessity," "inability" and "impossibility" should be given a prominent place.) Before children reach years of discretion, they can form no ideas of moral beings or of social relations: we ought therefore as far as possible to avoid using words which express such ideas, for fear that children should in early life attach false senses to them, which we cannot afterwards eradicate. The first false idea which a child forms is the germ of error and vice. It is to this first step that we must pay particular attention. See that he is affected only by sensible objects and that all his ideas are limited to his sensations: let him perceive nothing about him but the material world; otherwise be sure either that he will not listen to you or that he will form such fantastic notions of that moral world of which you tell him as you will never be able to efface all the days of his life.

e. No Reasoning with Children.

Locke's great maxim was to reason with children; and it is the most popular method at the present day. Its success does not appear to recommend it; for my own part, I have never seen anyone so silly as those children with whom they have reasoned so much. Of all man's faculties, Reason, which is a combination of the rest, is developed last and with greatest difficulty; yet this is the faculty which we are asked to use for the development of the earlier. It is the climax of a good education to form a man who is capable of reason; and we propose to educate a young child by means of his reason! This is beginning where we ought to end, and making of the finished product an instrument in its own manufacture. . . .

We may reduce almost all the moral instruction which has been or can be given to children to the following formula. "You must not do that." "Why not?" "Because it's naughty." "What does naughty mean?" "Doing what you are told not to do." "What harm is there in doing what you are told not to do?" "You will be punished for your disobedience." "Then I shall do it so that no-one finds out." "You will be watched." "I shall hide." "You will be asked." "I shall tell a story." "But you must not tell stories." "Why not?" "Because it is naughty." "Why is it naughty?" The circle is inevitable; if we go away from it, the child no longer understands us. . . . In striving to persuade your pupils to regard obedience as a duty, you always add to this pretended persuasion the force of compulsion or threats, or (what is worse) enforce it by flattery and promises. While they are really enticed by interest or constrained by violence, they pretend to be convinced by reason. . . .[1]

f. Education Negative.

Do not command your pupil to do anything in the world—absolutely nothing. Do not let him even imagine that you claim any authority over him. Let him know only that he is weak and that you are strong; that from your respective situations he necessarily lies at your mercy; let him learn it, let him know it, let him feel it; let him from the first feel on his proud neck the hard yoke which Nature has imposed on man, the heavy yoke of necessity, a yoke which is fashioned by the nature of things and not by the caprices of men. Let the bridle which constrains him be compulsion, not authority. In case of acts which he ought not to perform, do not forbid him—prevent him, without explanation, without argument. . . . By this method you will make him patient, even-tempered, resigned, and well-behaved, even when he is not indulged in his inclinations: it is our nature to endure patiently the necessity of things but not the unkindness of our fellows. "It is all gone" is an answer in face of which a child never complains if he believes it to be true. After all, there is no middle course; we must either exact nothing or subject him from the first to the most rigid obedience. The very worst education is to keep a child wavering between his own will and yours, to be eternally disputing which shall be master. I had a hundred times rather let him invariably have his own way.

[1] *Vide* also pp. 27, 28.

It is strange that, ever since men have engaged in the education of children, they should never have thought of any other means to effect their purpose but emulation, jealousy, envy, vanity, greed, and servile fear, all passions the most dangerous, the most apt to ferment, and the most liable to corrupt the soul, even before the body is formed. With every premature instruction which we instil into the head, we implant a vice in the depths of the heart. Senseless preceptors! who think they are doing marvels when, in order to teach children the theory of virtue, they drive them to the practice of vice! And then they actually tell us, Such is man! Yes, such is the man whom *you* make.

Every method has been tried but one, the only one which can succeed—well-regulated liberty. No-one should undertake the education of a child who cannot lead him where he wishes merely by the laws of possibility and impossibility. The spheres of both are equally unknown to the child; we may extend or contract them as we please. Necessity is the one stimulus and the one restraint at which he will never murmur. Natural compulsion is the one power which will make him pliant and tractable without sowing the seeds of vice in his heart: the passions will never be vigorous so long as they produce no effect. Give your pupil no lesson in words; he must learn only from experience. Inflict on him no kind of punishment; for he does not know what it means to be in fault. Never make him ask your pardon; for he cannot offend you. As he is devoid of all morality in his actions, he cannot do anything morally wrong or deserving of punishment or censure. . . .

Let us lay it down as an incontestible maxim that the first promptings of nature are always right. There is no original corruption in the human heart : there is not a

single vice to be found there of which one could not say
how and by what means it entered The only passion
natural to man is self-love (*amour de soi*) or egoism (*amour
propre*) taken in an extended sense. This passion,
considered in itself, that is as relative to the individual,
is good and useful; and, as it has no necessary relation
to anyone else, it is in its nature indifferent : it becomes
good or bad only from the application which we make of
it and the relations which we give it. Up to the appearance, therefore, of the faculty which regulates this self-
love, that is of Reason, a child should do nothing because
he is seen or heard, in a word nothing that implies a
relation to others, but only what is required by Nature ;
he will then do nothing wrong.

[He may do damage, but without any bad intention.
It is best to keep him in plain surroundings and, if he
does break anything, to act precisely as if it had broken
of itself.]

May I venture to lay down the greatest, the most
important, and the most useful rule of all education ? It
is this, *not to gain time but to lose it.* I beg my readers
to excuse my paradoxes; there is need of them in making
reflections; and, say what you will, I had rather be a
man of paradoxes than a man of prejudices. The most
critical period of human life is that between our birth
and the age of twelve. This is the time when vice and
error take root without our possessing any instrument
with which to destroy them : and, when the instrument
is found, they are so firmly fixed that they can no longer
be eradicated. If children took a leap from their
mother's breast to the age of reason, the ordinary
education might be very suitable; but, in the actual
order, they require one that is quite the opposite.

Children should not use their intellect till it has acquired all its faculties. . . . The first education therefore should be purely negative. It consists, not in teaching virtue or truth, but in guarding the heart from vice and the mind from error. If you could do nothing and prevent anything being done, if you could bring up your pupil strong and healthy to the age of twelve without his being able to distinguish his right hand from his left, then from the first the eyes of his understanding would be open to reason; without habit or prejudice, he would have within him nothing which could counteract your efforts, and he would, under your care, become the wisest of men. By attempting nothing in the beginning, you would have produced an educational prodigy.

Take the path directly opposite to that which is in use and you will almost always do right. . . . Exercise his body, his organs, his senses, his faculties; but keep his mind inactive as long as possible. Be cautious of all sentiments which he acquires previous to the judgment which can weigh them. . . . Whatever instruction is necessary, take care not to give it to-day, if it may without danger be deferred till to-morrow.

Another consideration which confirms the utility of this method is the child's particular disposition, which ought to be known before you can judge what moral regimen is best adapted to it. . . . A prudent tutor will observe his pupil well before he speaks the first word; he will first leave his natural character perfect liberty to unfold; he will lay him under no restraint that he may better learn his entire character.

[The tutor should set a good example: still——] Children are less corrupted by the bad examples which they see than by the bad precepts which you teach them. Always moralizing, sententious, pedantic, for every single idea which you believe to be good, you instil at the same time twenty others which are undoubtedly bad!

Only listen to one of these young gentlemen who have been thus lectured; let him talk, ask questions, and chatter freely, you will be surprised to find what a strange turn your fine reasonings have taken in his mind : he confuses all you have said, he reverses everything ; he will tire out your patience and almost distract you by his unexpected objections. He will either reduce you to silence or compel you to impose silence on him ; and what can he think of the silence of a man who loves talking so much ? If once he gains this advantage and realizes it, good-bye to education; all is at an end at once, he will henceforth seek opportunities, not to instruct himself, but to refute you.

[If Émile sees a man in a towering passion, we are to tell him that the poor man is ill.]

g. Moral Teaching through Action.

I do not consider it to be possible, in the midst of society, to bring up a child to the age of twelve without giving him any idea of the relations of man to man or of the morality of human actions. It is enough to postpone the appearance of these inevitable ideas as long as possible and, when they can be postponed no longer, to confine them to objects of immediate utility. It is enough to prevent him from thinking himself master of the world and injuring others without scruple and without intent. . . .

Our first obligations concern ourselves. . . . Hence our first sense of justice arises, not from what we owe to others, but from what they owe to us. . . . The first notion therefore which must be given to [an overbearing] child is not that of liberty but that of property. In order to give him this idea, he must own something. To speak of his clothes, his furniture, or his playthings, is useless; although they are at his disposal, he does not know how or why he is possessed of them. To tell him that they are his because they have been given to him is equally useless; for, in order to give them to him, some-one must already own them, and it is the very beginning of ownership which we wish to explain to him. . . . It is therefore necessary to go back to the origin of property; this is the source from which his first ideas on the subject should be taken. My pupil, as he lives in the country, has of course gained some notion of husbandry; he needs only eyes and leisure for that purpose, and he possesses both. People of all ages, but children above all, wish to show signs of their power and activity by imitation, creation, and production. Émile has not twice seen the cultivation of the garden and sowing and growth of beans, before he wishes to be a gardener himself. In accordance with my general principle, I do not oppose his wish; on the contrary, I encourage him, share his tastes, and work with him—not to please him but to please myself, at least he thinks so. . . . He takes possession of the soil by planting a bean. . . . We come every day to water our beans and are delighted to see them spring up. I increase his pleasure by telling him that this spot *belongs* to him. In explaining this word I make him feel that he has spent his time, his work, his trouble, in short his whole person upon it, that he has in this plot a part of himself, which he may keep against all comers, just as he might wrest his arm out of the hands of anyone who wished to hold it against his will.

One day, he comes in a hurry, his water-can in his hand. What a sight! His beans are all torn up by the roots, the ground is turned up, and the place is hardly recognizable. " Oh! what is become of my toil and pains, the fruit of all my work and industry ?   Who has deprived me of my property ?   Who has taken away my beans ?"   His young heart throbs; the first sense of injustice stings him; his tears flow in torrents; he fills the air with his cries and complaints.   I share his indignation and distress, and try to discover the author of the mischief.   It is found to be the gardener.   We send for him.   But the result is a surprise.   As soon as he understand our grievance, he begins to complain louder than we.   " So, gentlemen, it is you who have spoiled my work!   I had sown some fine Maltese melons there; the seed was given me as a curiosity ;   I was hoping to give you a treat when they were ripe ;   and, just as they were springing up, you have dug them up to plant your wretched beans !   I can never replace them, and you have lost the pleasure of tasting some splendid melons." "Forgive us, my poor Robert, you had worked hard here. We have done wrong in spoiling your work : but we will send for some fresh seed and will not dig again till we have made sure that no-one has been at work on the same spot before."   " Then you may throw aside your tools, gentlemen; for there is no ground here uncultivated.   I work the ground which my father improved before me; we all do the same; all the land you see has been occupied long ago."   Émile : " Is melon-seed often destroyed, Mr. Robert ?"   " Excuse me, young gentleman, we do not often meet with such wild little gardeners as you.   With us, no-one meddles with other people's gardens ; we respect their work so that they shall not interfere with ours."   " But I have no garden."   "What has that to do with me ?   If you spoil mine, I shall not let you walk in it any more; you see, I don't want to throw my time away." "Can't we make an arrangement with kind Robert? Supposing he gave us a corner of his garden to ourselves on condition that we give him half the produce." "I will give you a corner without any conditions; but remember that I shall dig up your beans if you meddle with my melons. . . ." From this point it is but a single step to the theory of property and exchange; there he must stop. . . .

Think of this example, my young preceptors; and remember that your lessons should always consist rather of action than of words : children easily forget what is said to them and what they say themselves, but not what they do or what is done to them.

h. Discipline of Natural Consequences.

He breaks the windows of his room. Let the wind blow in day and night; do not mind his catching cold. It is better that he should catch cold than that he should do such silly things. Never complain of the inconvenience which he is causing you; but contrive that he may be the first to feel it. At last you have the windows mended, but without saying anything to him. Should he break them again, you change your method. You say to him very coldly but without anger, "These windows are mine; I had them put there, and I want to make sure that they are not broken." Then you shut him up in a dark room without windows. At the novelty of this proceeding, he will begin to cry and storm; no one listens. Soon he grows tired and changes his tone; he sighs and groans. A servant happens to pass; he asks to be let out. The servant does not make an excuse for not complying, but observes, "I too have windows to protect," and walks away. After the child has remained there some hours, long enough to tire him heartily and make him remember it, someone will suggest his making you a proposal to let him out on condition of his breaking no more windows. . . . You go; you hear his proposal and instantly accept it. "What a good idea! What a pity you did not think of it sooner! We shall both be gainers by it." Without requiring any protestations or confirmation of his promise, you embrace him and take him back at once to his room. . . .

I have said enough to make it clear that I would never have punishment inflicted on children as punishment; it should follow as a natural consequence of their misdeeds. Hence you will never declaim against lying, nor punish them directly for telling untruths; but you will contrive that they feel the ill effects of lying, by not being believed when they speak the truth, and by being accused of acts of which they are innocent in spite of all their protests. . . .

Falsehoods are of two kinds, false statements concerning the past and false promises with regard to the future. . . . [As regards the first] it is the law of obedience which produces the necessity for lying, because obedience is painful and children secretly try to escape it. . . . If you never punish or scold him and never demand anything from him, why should he not tell you all he has done as openly as he tells any of his little companions? . . . [As regards the second] a child can hardly be said to deceive when he makes a promise; for he thinks of nothing but how to escape from some immediate difficulty. If he could escape a whipping or obtain a box of sweets by promising to throw himself out of window the next day, he would promise on the spot. . . . It follows that children's lies must be attributed to their masters, and that trying to teach them to tell the truth is the same thing as teaching them to tell lies. . . . For my own part, as I give my pupil only practical lessons and had rather see him good than learned, I never try to find out the truth from him for fear lest he should disguise it, and never exact any promise from him for fear lest he should be tempted to break it. . . . If his intractable disposition ever compels me to enter into any agreement with him, I shall take my measures so well that the proposal shall always come from him and not from me; that, when he has once promised, he shall always see a real and immediate interest in keeping his promise; and that, if he ever fails to do so, the ill consequences shall appear to rise naturally from the order and constitution of things and not from the resentment of his tutor.

i. Imitation and Habit.

Appearing to preach virtue, we make children love vice; we implant it in the act of forbidding it. To make them religious, we tire out their patience at church, and, by making them perpetually mutter prayers, we make them sigh for the time when they will pray no longer. To teach them charity, we make them give alms, as if we were above doing it ourselves. It is the master who should give alms, not the pupil; he should make him believe that a child of his age is not yet worthy of so great a privilege. . . .

Notice that we only accustom children to give away things of which they do not know the value. Of what value to them are the pieces of metal which they carry in their pockets, which serve no other purpose but to give away? A child would sooner give a beggar a hundred guineas than a cake; but require the little prodigal to give away his toys, his sweets, or other trifles for which he really cares and you will soon see whether you have made him truly liberal.

A further expedient has been discovered, that of promptly returning to children whatever they give away. . . . Locke advises us to convince children by experience that the most liberal is always the best provided for. This plan makes a child liberal in appearance and covetous in fact. He adds that children will thus acquire a habit of liberality. Yes, the liberality of a usurer, who gives a penny to get a pound. But when it comes to be a question of giving away in earnest, farewell to the habit; when we stop giving back, they will soon stop giving away. We should regard the habit of mind, not that of the hand. . . .

Masters, away with your tricks! Be virtuous and good yourselves, that your examples may be engraved in the memory of your pupils, till in time they sink into their hearts. Instead of hastening to require my pupil to perform acts of charity, I would rather perform them myself in his presence and deprive him of the means of imitating me, as being an honour too great for his years; for it is important that he should not regard the obligations of men merely as those of children. . . . I should at least prevent him from doing it ostentatiously; I should prefer his usurping my privilege, and giving away his money by stealth. Such a piece of fraud would be compatible with his age and the only one which I should forgive him.

I know that the imitative virtues are but the virtues of an ape, and that no action is morally good which is not performed as such, and not merely because it is performed by others. But at so early an age, while the heart is still insensible, children ought to be led to imitate those actions of which we wish them to acquire a habit, until they are able to perform them from principle and from a love of virtue. Man is an imitative being; so are animals; this tendency is good as ordained by Nature, but degenerates into vice in society. . . .

The only lesson of morality suitable to children, and the most important for persons of all ages, is never to do an injury to anyone. Even the positive precept to do good, if not made subordinate to the former, is dangerous, false, and contradictory. Who is there that does not do good? Everyone does good, the vicious as much as the virtuous; he will make one person happy at the expense of making a hundred miserable—that is the source of all our troubles! The most sublime virtues are negative; they are also the most difficult, because they are attended with no ostentation. . . .

j. Passage from a later Part of the Book.

In the careful method of education, the master commands and thinks that he governs, whereas it is, in fact, the pupil who governs the master. A child uses the tutor's requirements to obtain his own wishes: he always knows how to obtain eight hours' indulgence for one hour's work. . . . Take a contrary method with your pupil; let him always believe himself to be master, and always be master yourself. There is no subjection so complete as that which preserves the appearance of liberty; it is by this means that even the will is led captive. The poor child, who knows nothing, who can do nothing, who is acquainted with nothing, is surely at your mercy. Do you not arrange his whole environment? Can you not cause him pleasure or pain just as you please? His work, his games, his pleasures, his pains, are they not all in your hands without his knowing it? Certainly, he should do only what he wishes, but he should only wish what you desire, he should not take a step which you have not foreseen nor open his lips to speak without your knowing what he is about to say.

[Rousseau then gives two stories from his own experience; how he succeeded by passive resistance with a child who tried to make him get out of bed to bring him a light, and how with a pupil who would not go a walk one day he refused to go out the next.]

2. Intellectual and Physical Training.

a. Postponement of Ordinary Book-learning.

Mothers take for extraordinary signs the most usual and ordinary tokens, such as vivacity, flashes of humour, playfulness, and a subtle simplicity, which are characteristic of their years and prove that a child is but a child. . . . Treat him therefore according to his age in spite of appearances, and beware of exhausting his strength by an unreasonable desire to see him exert it. . . . Forward children make ordinary men. Nothing is harder than to distinguish between real stupidity and that apparent dulness which is an indication of a strong intellect. . . .

But you are alarmed at seeing a child spend his early years doing nothing. What! Is it nothing to be happy? Dancing, playing, and running about all day—are these nothing? He will never be so busy all his life. [The authority of Plato and Seneca is then quoted.]

The apparent ease with which children learn operates greatly to their prejudice; and, though we fail to notice it, is a plain proof that they learn nothing. The delicate texture of their brains reflects like a mirror every object which is presented to them; but nothing penetrates or is left behind. A child retains the words, but the ideas are reflected back; the hearer may understand, but he himself understands nothing.

Though Memory and Reason are entirely different faculties, the former cannot really develop without the latter. Till a child reaches years of understanding, he does not receive ideas, but only images. Images are merely direct copies of sensible objects; ideas are notions of objects as determined by their relations. An image may exist in isolation in the percipient mind, but every idea presupposes others. Imagery is only artificial seeing; conception involves comparison. Our sensations are purely passive, whereas ideas arise from an active principle which is capable of forming judgments.

I say therefore that children, being incapable of forming judgments, have no real memory. They retain sounds, shapes, and sensations, but rarely ideas, and still more rarely the connexions between them. It is sometimes urged as an objection to this view that children may be taught certain elements of geometry The instance really supports me. It may be shown that, so far from reasoning themselves, they cannot even retain the arguments of others. Examine the method of these little geometers and you will see that they retain only the exact impression of the figure and the exact words of the proof. On the least unforeseen objection, they are quite at a loss; vary the figure and they are totally disconcerted; all their knowledge lies in their sensations, nothing has penetrated into the understanding. Their very memory is as little perfected as their other faculties; they are almost always obliged in later life to learn the reality which corresponds to the words memorized in childhood.

I am, however, far from thinking that children are capable of no kind of reasoning. On the contrary, I observe that they reason excellently on matters with which they are acquainted and which concern their present and obvious interest. It is in the extent of their knowledge that we deceive ourselves; we attribute to them knowledge which they do not possess and set them to reason about things which they cannot understand. We are still further mistaken in wishing to make them attend to considerations which can in no degree affect them, such as their future interest, or their happiness and reputation when they grow to manhood—arguments which, to beings who are devoid of all foresight, signify absolutely nothing. Thus all the studies which are imposed on these poor unfortunates relate to aims entirely foreign to their minds. Judge, then, of the attention which they are likely to bestow on them!

The pedagogues who make such a parade of the instruction which they give their pupils are paid to talk in a different strain; you can, however, plainly see by their conduct that they are quite of my opinion; for, after all, what do they teach? Words, always words, and nothing but words. Among the various branches of knowledge which they claim to teach, they take particular care not to choose any which would really be useful to their pupils, because these would involve a knowledge of things, which they could never succeed in giving. They therefore choose those which a child appears to understand when he knows the terms—geography, chronology, heraldry, languages—studies so foreign to the purposes of man, and especially of a child, that it would be a marvel if he had a single occasion to use them.

It may be a surprise that I reckon the study of languages among the useless branches of education; but it should be remembered that I am here speaking of the studies of childhood; and, whatever may be said to the contrary, I very much doubt whether any child, prodigies excepted, has ever really learned two languages before the age of twelve or fifteen.

I agree that, if the study of languages were only a study of words, that is to say, of the letters and sounds that serve as symbols, it would be a suitable study for children. But languages, in changing the symbols, modify also the ideas which those symbols represent. Our ideas are based on our language; our thoughts take a tincture of our idioms. Judgments of fact alone correspond; turns of thought take a particular form in each language. This difference may well be in part the cause or effect of national characteristics. This conjecture appears to be confirmed by the fact that, among all nations in the world, language follows the fortunes of manners, and is preserved or corrupted as they are. Of these various forms of thinking and speaking, a child becomes habituated to one, and that is the only one which he possesses up to the age of reason. In order to acquire two, he must be able to compare ideas; and how can he compare what he is hardly able to form? He might learn a thousand different names for every object, but every idea will have but one form. He can therefore only learn to speak one language. Shall I be told that children actually learn several? I deny the fact: I have seen little prodigies who believed that they could talk five or six: I have heard them use successively a Latin, a French and an Italian vocabulary—to talk German! Give a child as many synonyms as you like, you will change only his words, not his language. He will never know more than one.

It is to conceal children's incapacity in this respect that teachers prefer the use of dead languages, of which there are no longer any recognized judges. The common use of these languages being long lost, they are content to imitate what they find written in books; and this they call speaking the language. If such be the Latin and Greek of the masters, imagine that of their pupils! No sooner have they learned their accidence by heart, without understanding a word, than they are set to turn a passage of French into a Latin vocabulary. When they are a little more advanced, they are made to patch up a prose "theme" by tacking together phrases of Cicero, or a set of verses with "tags" of Vergil. They then think that they are able to speak Latin, and who is there to contradict them?

In any study whatever, unless we possess the ideas of the things represented, the symbolic signs are valueless. A child is nevertheless always confined to the signs, though we can never make him understand the things which they represent. Thus, while we imagine that we are giving him a description of the earth, we are only teaching him to recognize a map; we teach him the names of countries, towns, and rivers, but he does not realize that they exist elsewhere than on the paper. I remember once seeing a geography book which began, "What is the world? A pasteboard globe." This is exactly the geography of children: for I lay it down as certain that there is no child of ten, though he has spent two years in the study of cosmography and the use of the globes, who can tell by the rules which he has learned how to find his way from Paris to St. Denis. Nay, I will venture to say, there is not one who, by means of a plan of his father's garden, could follow the walks without losing himself. Such are these learned geographers who can tell the exact position of Pekin, Ispahan, Mexico, and all the countries of the globe!

By a still more ridiculous error children are made to study history. It is imagined that history is within their capacity because it is only a collection of facts. But what is meant by facts? Is it supposed that the relations which determine historical facts are so easily grasped that ideas of these relations are formed without trouble in children's minds? Is it supposed that a true knowledge of events can be separated from that of their causes and effects, or that history is so little connected with morality that the one can be understood without the other? If you see nothing more in the actions of men than external and physical operations, what can you learn from history? Absolutely nothing. It would lose all interest, it would afford neither pleasure nor instruction. On the other hand, if you wish to estimate actions by their moral relations try to give your pupils an idea of those relations and you will soon see whether the study of history is within the capacity of children. . . .

[During a stay at a country-house] I happened one morning to be present at the lessons of the elder child. The tutor, who had instructed his pupil very well in ancient history, in telling the life of Alexander came to the well-known story of his physician Philip.[1] . . . At dinner, according to the French custom, the young man was encouraged to chatter. The vivacity of his age and the certainty of applause made him throw out a number of silly remarks; among which now and then some happy idea made them forget the rest. At last came the story of the physician, which he related very clearly and gracefully. . . . After dinner, suspecting from several indications that my young doctor did not understand it

[1] Alexander, being informed by letter that Philip had been bribed by Darius to poison him, gave the letter to Philip as he drank the potion which the latter presented to him.

in the least, I took him by the hand and, taking a walk in the park, where I could talk to him freely, I found that he admired the boasted courage of Alexander more than any of the company; but can you guess in what he thought that this courage consisted? Merely in swallowing at one draught a disagreeable medicine without hesitating or showing any disgust. The poor boy, who had been obliged to take medicine not a fortnight before and had swallowed it only after great efforts, had still the taste of it in his mouth. Death and poisoning had been reduced in his mind to disagreeable sensations; he could conceive no other poison than a draught of senna. . . .

If Nature has given to children's brains a pliability which enables them to receive all kinds of impressions, it is not with a view that we should imprint thereon the names of kings, dates, heraldic devices, astronomical or geographical terms, and all those words, meaningless to children and useless to men, with which we burden their sad and empty childhood. Rather is it that useful and comprehensible ideas, ideas which relate to their happiness and will one day throw light on their duties, may be so engraved on their minds at an early age in indelible characters, that they may help them to regulate their whole life in a manner which shall be suitable both to their condition and to their faculties.

The kind of memory which children possess may be fully employed without setting them to study books. Everything they see or hear strikes their fancy and is retained in their memories. They keep in their minds a register of the actions and conversation of men; their whole environment is the book from which, without conscious effort, they are constantly enriching their memory against the time when their judgment will be able to profit by it. It is in the choice of these objects, in the constant presentation of those which they can understand, and the concealment of those which they should overlook, that real skill in cultivating this primary faculty consists.   It is by such means that we should try to form a store of knowledge which will serve to educate them during youth and to regulate their conduct all their lives. . . .

Émile will never learn anything by heart, not even fables, not even those of La Fontaine, simple and beautiful as they are; for the words of fables are no more fables than the words of a history book are history.

How can we be so blind as to think fables a moral training for children, without reflecting that the moral, while amusing, only deceives them, and that, charmed by the fiction, they miss the underlying truth?   Fables may instruct adults, but the naked truth must be presented to children.

All children learn La Fontaine's fables, not one understands them.   Could they understand them, the case would be still worse; for the moral is so complicated and so far above their capacities that it would rather incline them to vice than to virtue.   [He chooses the first fable as an instance.]

THE RAVEN AND THE FOX.

Master Raven, perched in the trees,

Master!   What does the word mean in itself?   What does it mean before a proper name?   What is the particular meaning here?   What is a raven?

Held in his beak a fine big cheese.

What kind of cheese?   Swiss or Dutch?   If a child has never seen a raven, what do you gain by talking to him about them?   If he has, how can he imagine that it

could hold a cheese in its beak? Our descriptions
should always accord with nature.

Master Fox, allured by the smell,

Master again! but this time it is a good title—he is a
past master in the arts of his profession. We must
explain what a fox is and distinguish between his true
nature and the conventional character which is given
him in fables. *Alleché* (allured) is an obsolete word
used only in verse; a child will ask why we talk
differently in verse and in prose. What answer will you
make? "Allured by the smell of a cheese!" This
cheese, held by a raven perched in a tree, must have had
a very strong smell to be scented by a fox lurking in a
thicket or a burrow. Is this the way in which you train
your pupil to a spirit of judicious criticism which will
not allow him to be imposed on and will enable him to
distinguish truth from falsehood in the statements of
others?

Thus he begins his tale to tell.

Do foxes talk, then? And do they speak the same
language as ravens? Take care, my wise teacher;
consider well before you answer. It is of more consequence than you think.

" Ha, Mr. Raven! I wish you good day!

So Mr. is a title which the child hears turned into
ridicule before he knows that it is a mark of respect.

What feathers you have! What a fine display!

Wretchedly expletive and redundant! A child, hearing the same thing repeated in different words, will learn
a loose method of speaking.

I tell no lies ; if only your note

"I tell no lies": then do people sometimes tell lies? But what will your pupil think if you tell him that the fox says this only because he actually is telling the raven a lie?

At all corresponded to yon fine coat,

"Corresponded": what does this mean? Try to teach a child to compare two qualities so different as plumage and singing, and you will find how far he can understand you.

A phœnix you'ld be mid the forest lords,

"A phœnix": what is a phœnix? We are suddenly landed in the fictions of antiquity, almost in mythology. "Forest lords": what a figurative expression! The flatterer raises his language and gives it more dignity in order to render it more seductive. How is a child to understand this finesse? Does he know, is it possible that he should know, the difference between an elevated and a common style?

And, out of his wits with joy at his words,

A child must have already experienced very lively and strong passions to be able to comprehend this proverbial mode of expression.

The Raven, his beautiful voice to display,

It must not be forgotten that, in order to understand this verse and the whole fable, a child must already know the " beautiful voice" of the raven.

He opes his large beak and lets fall his prey.

The verse is admirable; the sound and sense correspond. I can imagine I see the wide beak open and hear the cheese rattle through the boughs ; but this kind of beauty is lost on children.

The Fox snapped it up : " My good Sir," said he,

Good Sir ! See goodness already made fun of ! Assuredly there is no loss of time in instructing children !

Flatterers always, you thus may see,

A general maxim ! They will not understand !

Live at the cost of those they squeeze ;

No child of ten can understand this line.

This lesson no doubt is worth a cheese."

This line is intelligible and the thought is good. But there are few children who can compare a lesson with a cheese and would not prefer the cheese. They must be taught therefore that this is only a piece of raillery. What subtilty for children !

Too late the Raven, in sorrow and pain,

Another pleonasm, for which there is no excuse.

Swore that he'ld ne'er be cajoled again.

" Swore." Where is the tutor foolish enough to explain to a child what swearing means ?

I ask if it is to children of six that it is proper to teach that there are men who flatter and deceive for gain. At most we might teach them that there are jesters who praise little boys to their faces and laugh at their childish vanity behind their backs : but the cheese spoils all ; and they learn less how to prevent it falling from their own mouths than how to make it fall from the mouths of others. This is another paradox and not the least important.

Watch children learning fables and you will find that, when they are capable of applying them, they almost always do so contrary to the intention of the author: instead of remarking the error from which you wish to keep them, they fall in love with the vice which profits by it. In the fable above cited, children laugh at the raven but love the fox. . . . In all fables where a lion is introduced, as he is generally the most conspicuous character, a child never fails to assume the part of lion; and, when he presides at any distribution, he profits by his model and takes the lion's share. But when the gnat stings the lion, it is another matter; the child is then no longer the lion but the gnat, and learns how he may some day kill with a pin prick those whom he dare not attack openly.

[Other instances are then quoted.]

In thus relieving children from all obligations, I free them from their greatest source of misery, namely books. Reading is the scourge of childhood, yet it is usually the only occupation that is given. At twelve years of age Émile will hardly know what a book is. But you will say, "Surely he ought at least to learn to read." Yes, he shall learn to read when reading will be of any use to him; till then, it only serves to disgust him.

If nothing is to be required of children from obedience, it follows that they will learn nothing of which they do not perceive the actual and immediate advantage either for use or for amusement; for what other motive will induce them to learn? The art of speaking to persons who are absent, of understanding them in turn, of communicating to those who are at a great distance our sentiments, our inclinations, and desires; this is an art of which the utility may be made known to the simplest understanding. Whence then comes it that so useful and agreeable an art has become such a torment to children? The reason is plain; it is because they are compelled to learn, whether they will or no; and because it is applied to uses which they cannot understand. A child is not very anxious to perfect the instrument by which he is tormented. Only make this instrument minister to his pleasures and he will soon apply himself to it, whether you wish it or not

Great efforts have been made to find out the best method of teaching children to read; cards and presses have been invented, they have turned the nursery into a printer's shop. Locke would have reading taught with letters carved on dice. Is not this an excellent device? A waste of energy! A more certain incentive than any, which is nevertheless always neglected, is the wish to learn. Give a child the wish and do as you will about cards and dice; any method will then be suitable.

The grand motive, the only motive which leads him far ahead with certainty, is present interest. Émile sometimes receives written invitations from his father, relatives, and friends, to dinner, to go for a walk, to a boating picnic, or to some entertainment. These invitations are short, plain, precise, and clearly written. He must find someone to read them to him. Such a person is not always at hand at the right moment, or is as disobliging to the child as the child was to him the day before. The chance is lost; the letter is read to him afterwards, but it is too late. If only he could have read it himself! He receives others; they are so short! and so interesting! He would like to try to make them out. Sometimes he is helped: sometimes help is refused. He struggles on, and at last makes out half of a letter He is invited to go out to-morrow to eat cream: but cannot find out where or with whom. How many efforts will he not make to find out the rest! I do not think Émile will need a press I might here speak of teaching him to write; but I am ashamed of diverting myself with such trivialities in a treatise on *education*

I will only add one word more. It is an important maxim—children generally acquire speedily and certainly whatever they are not pressed to learn. I am almost certain that Émile will know perfectly well how to read and write before he is ten, precisely because I care very little whether he learn before he is fifteen: but I had much sooner that he should never learn to read at all than that he should acquire the power at the expense of everything that would make it of use to him; and of what use will be his knowing how to read if he has taken a dislike to books for ever?

b. Dependence of Intellectual on Physical Training.

If you proceed on the plan which I have begun to sketch and follow rules directly contrary to those which are commonly received; if you no longer carry your pupil's thoughts to a distance and make him ceaselessly wander in strange countries, climates, and ages; if, instead of transferring him to the extremities of the earth and even to the skies, you keep his attention fixed on himself and his immediate surroundings; you will then find him capable of perception, of memory, and even of reason : this is the order of Nature. In proportion as a sensitive being becomes active, he acquires a discernment proportionate to his strength; it is only when he possesses more strength than is necessary for his preservation that he develops those speculative faculties which are adapted to the employment of his capacity to other purposes. If therefore you wish to train your pupil's understanding,

train the capacities which it is to control. Keep him
in constant bodily exercise; bring him up robust and
healthy, to make him reasonable and wise : let him work,
let him be active, let him run about, let him make a noise,
in short let him always be in motion. Once make him a
man in vigour, and he will soon become a man in understanding. . . .

There are two kinds of men who live in constant bodily
exercise and think equally little of the cultivation of
their minds—peasants and savages. Peasants are dull,
clownish and stupid; savages are remarkable for their
strong sense and keenness of intellect. Whence comes
this difference ? The peasant, always doing what he is
bidden, or what he has seen his father do, or what he has
done from his youth, never acts except by rote; and, as
he is little better than a machine, and is constantly
employed on the same tasks, habit and obedience usurp
the place of reason. With the savage, the case is
different; being attached to no one place, having no
settled task, obedient to no-one, and restrained by no
other law but his own will, he is obliged to reason upon
every action of his life; he never makes a movement or
takes a step without having first considered the consequences. Thus, the more his body is exercised, the more
is his mind enlightened; his mental and bodily powers
advance together, and mutually improve each other.

Let us see, my prudent tutor, which of our pupils most
resembles the savage and which the peasant. Yours,
subjected in everything to an authority which is always
directing him, does nothing but what he is bidden . . .
for why do you expect him to think when you always
think for him ? . . . My pupil, or rather the pupil of
Nature, being from an early stage compelled to provide
as much as possible for himself, is not obliged to apply

continually to others, much less to make a display of his great learning.   To compensate, he judges, foresees, and reasons concerning everything which relates to his own interest.   He does not prate, he acts; he knows nothing of what is being done in the world, but he knows very well how to do all that he needs.   As he is perpetually in motion, he is obliged to observe much and to note a variety of effects; he acquires an early and extensive experience, though his lessons come from Nature and not from men; he learns all the more because nowhere does he detect any plan for his instruction. . . .

Young tutor, I am teaching you a very different art, that of regulating without precepts and of doing everything by doing nothing.

[Here comes the passage quoted above as 1. *j.*, p. 107.]

The first time in my life that I went out of Geneva, I tried to keep up with a horse at full gallop, and threw stones at Mont de Salève two leagues off: I was laughed at by all the children in the village and appeared to them as a real idiot. At eighteen we are taught the use of the lever as a part of mechanics; in the country there is not a boy of twelve who does not understand it better than the first physicists in the Academy of Science. The lessons which schoolboys learn of one another in the playground are a hundred times more useful to them than any which they will ever say in class.

Watch a cat, the first time it comes into a room. It looks about and peers into every hole and corner; it is not still for a moment till it has carefully examined everything in the room. A child does the same when he begins to walk. . . . Our first impulses urge us to measure ourselves with our environment, to discover in objects any sensible qualities which might concern us.

Men's first study is a sort of experimental physical science relative to self-preservation. . . . While children's supple and delicate organs can adjust themselves to the physical world, while their senses are still exempt from illusions— this is the time to train these senses and organs in their proper functions, this is the time to teach them to recognize the sensible relations of things to themselves. As everything that enters the human mind comes through the senses, the first kind of reasoning in man is a kind of sensational reasoning, which serves as a basis for intellectual reason. Our first instructors in science are our feet, hands, and eyes. . . .

c. Clothing, Sleep, Exercise.

[Tight clothes and costly clothes are to be avoided.]

We not only see fond mothers promising their children fine clothes as a reward, but often hear foolish tutors threatening their pupils with coarser and plainer clothes as a punishment. . . . Is not this as much as to tell them, " Man is nothing but what his dress makes him; your worth is in your clothes." If I were obliged to correct a child who had been thus spoiled, I should take care that his richest clothes should be the most uncomfortable, that he should scarcely be able to stir or move in them, that his liberty and gaiety should be sacrificed to his magnificence.

[He should be lightly clad to suit an open-air life and wear no head-gear.]

Locke, amid a number of manly and sensible rules, falls into a contradiction which we should not expect in so exact a reasoner. Though advising that children should take cold baths in the heat of summer, he is against their drinking cold water when they are warm, or sitting on the damp ground. . . . I shall never be persuaded that our natural appetites are misguided, and that we may not satisfy them without endangering our lives. If this were really the case, the human race would have been destroyed hundreds of times before it had learned the precautions which were necessary for self-preservation.

[Spring water, however, should be warmed in summer.]

Children require much sleep because they take much exercise. . . . The time for rest is pointed out by nature as the night. It is a certain observation that our sleep is more tranquil and agreeable when the sun is below the horizon. . . . Hence the most healthy habit is certainly to rise and to go to bed with the sun; it follows that in this latitude man as well as animals requires in general more sleep in winter than in summer. But civilized life is not sufficiently simple and free from accident for us to think of accustoming a child to uniformity, to such an extent as to make it necessary for him. He ought without doubt to subject himself to rules; but the chief rule is to be able to break the others without risk when occasion requires. . . . Leave him at first without restraint to the law of nature; but never forget that in society we are obliged to put ourselves above that law. He must be able to sit up late and to rise early, to be waked unexpectedly out of sleep, and occasionally to sit up all night without inconvenience. By beginning early and by proceeding gently and gradually, we may thus train his constitution to bear conditions which might destroy it if he were subjected to them only after it has been already formed.

[He should be accustomed to sleep anywhere and on anything.]

I imagine that there is nothing for which we might not with a little address excite an inclination or even an ardent desire in children, without vanity, jealousy, or emulation. Their vivacity and turn for imitation will suffice, and particularly their native cheerfulness, by which we have always a sure hold over them, although no tutor has ever known how to make use of it. In all their games, as long as they are quite sure it is only play, they will suffer, without complaint and even with laughter, pains which would not otherwise have been borne without floods of tears. . . .

An exclusive education, intended only to distinguish persons so educated from the people, always prefers the most expensive accomplishments to the more common, which are also the most useful. Thus our carefully educated young people learn to ride, because it is expensive; but hardly any of them learn to swim, because it costs nothing. [Its utility is then discussed.]

d. Training of the Senses.

A child has neither the strength nor the judgment of a man; but he can see and hear as well, or nearly so. His palate is as sensitive, though less delicate; and he distinguishes odours equally well. Of all our faculties, the senses are the first to be developed and perfected: they are therefore the first that should be trained, whereas they are the most forgotten and neglected.

Training the senses implies more than merely exercising them; it means learning to use them in forming correct estimates, in short, *learning to perceive:* for we do not know how to touch, to see, or to hear, till we have learned.

Some exercises are purely physical and mechanical they serve to strengthen the body, without taking the least hold of the judgment; such are swimming, running, jumping, whipping a top, or throwing stones. These are excellent; but have we only arms and legs? Have we not also eyes and ears; and are not these organs necessary to the use of the former? Exercise therefore, not only your strength, but all the senses which direct it; make the best possible use of each, and let the impressions of one confirm those of another. Measure, count, weigh, compare. Exert your force only after you have estimated the resistance; let a forecast of the effect always precede the use of the means. Interest your pupil in never making superfluous or inadequate efforts. If you accustom him thus to foresee the effect of all his movements and to correct his mistakes by experience, is it not certain that, the more he acts, the better his judgment will become?

Let us suppose him about to move a heavy body; if he takes too long a lever, it will involve too much movement; if too short, he will not secure enough power; experience will teach him to choose precisely the right length. This kind of knowledge is not above his age. Is it a question of lifting a weight? If he would take up the heaviest he can carry and not try to raise one which he cannot, is he not obliged to estimate the weight by the eye? When he knows how to compare masses of the same material but of different bulk, let him choose between masses of the same bulk but of different material: he must for this purpose learn to compare their specific gravity. I remember a young man, very well educated, who could not be persuaded, till he had made the experiment, that a tub full of cleft wood was lighter than the same tub filled with water.

We are not equally expert in the use of all our senses.

There is one, the touch, whose action is never suspended
while we are awake. It is extended over the whole
surface of the body, and acts as a constant guard to
warn us of everything that might hurt us. It is through
this sense that, whether we will or no, we acquire our
earliest experience; we are constantly using it, and consequently we have less need to give it any particular
training. We find, however, that the blind have a much
stronger and more delicate sense of touch; because, receiving no information from the sight, they are obliged
to secure from the former sense alone the same conclusions which we obtain from the latter. Why are we not
trained to walk like them in the dark, to recognize the
bodies which we touch, to judge of surrounding objects,
in short to do by night without candles all which they
do by day without eyes? . . .

I would have a variety of diversions for the night.
This advice is more important than it appears. The
night naturally terrifies men, and sometimes animals.
Reason or knowledge, wisdom or courage deliver few
persons from paying this tribute. . . . This timidity
is usually attributed to nurses' tales. This is a mistake.
It has a natural cause, the same as that which makes the
deaf mistrustful and the ignorant superstitious; that is,
our ignorance of our surroundings and of what is passing
about us. . . . The cause of the evil being found, the
remedy is clearly indicated. Habit everywhere destroys
the effects of imagination; the latter is excited only by
novelty. . . . If therefore you wish to cure anyone of
this fear of darkness, do not reason with him, but entice
him often into the dark. Be sure that all the arguments
of philosophy will be of less avail than this practice. . . .
In order that these diversions should succeed, I cannot
recommend cheerfulness too strongly. Nothing is more

dismal than darkness; never shut up a child in a dungeon.
Let him go into the dark laughing, and come out again
laughing, in order that, while he is there, the thought of
the amusement which he has just left and to which he
is about to return may ward off those fantastic notions
which might otherwise intrude on his imagination.

[He then tells how he was sent to bring a Bible from
a church at night.]

I would make a kind of maze in a large room with
tables, chairs, stools and screens. In the tortuous
bends of this maze I would place eight or ten decoy
boxes and one, precisely similar, filled with sweets; I
would then describe in short and plain terms the exact
spot where this box was to be found; and, after making
the little competitors draw lots, send each in turn till
the prize is found.

[He opposes surprising children in the dark. Touch
is discussed again; Émile shall not wear boots. Perspective is very deceptive and training is necessary.]

We estimate heights, distances, depths, and magni-
tudes very inaccurately. A proof that this is not a
defect of the sense but of its use is that engineers,
surveyors, architects, masons, and painters have a better
eye for such matters than any other people, and estimate
dimensions and distances much more exactly. . . . It
is easy to prevail on children to engage in any occupation that requires them to move about freely. There
are a thousand ways to interest them in measuring and
estimating distances. Let us suppose we have a very
high cherry-tree; what must we do to gather some
cherries from the top? Is the ladder in the barn long
enough? Here is a stream too wide to jump. How

shall we get across? Will one of the planks in the court reach from side to side? We have a mind to fish in the moat from the window; how many fathoms must our line be? I want to make a swing between two trees; how many yards of rope are needed? They tell me that our room in the other house is to be five and twenty feet square; do you think it will be big enough for us? Is it bigger than this? We are very hungry and there are two villages in sight; at which shall we dine?

You wish to induce an indolent and lazy child to run, though he has no natural inclination for that, or any other, form of exercise. The difficulty would be all the greater, because I will not lay on him any command whatever. . . . In taking our walk after dinner, I sometimes used to put a couple of his favourite cakes in my pocket; we would each eat one, and return contentedly home. One day he noticed that I had three cakes. As he could easily eat half a dozen, he soon despatched his own and asked me for the third. "No," I said, "I can eat it very well myself, or we will divide it; or, stay, we had better let those two little boys run a race for it." I call them, show them the cake, and propose the terms. They desire nothing better; the cake is accordingly placed on a large stone which serves as winning-post. The distance being marked, we go and sit down; at the given signal, the boys set off; the winner seizes the cake and devours it without mercy before the eyes of the loser and the spectators. . . . Mortified at seeing his favourite cakes thus devoured by others before his eyes, my young gentleman at last begins to suspect that running is of some use; and, seeing that he has two legs as well as other boys, he begins to practise by himself. I take care not to observe him, but see that my device has succeeded. As soon as he thinks himself equal to the enterprise, he does what I expect and pretends to beg the remaining cake. Of course I refuse to give it; at which he seems annoyed. "Well, Sir," he says, "lay it down on the stone; mark the distance, and we will see." "Good," I reply laughing, "can so fine a gentleman as you run? You will only be more hungry, and will get nothing to eat." Piqued at my raillery, he exerts all his energy and carries off the prize; which is the easier as I have made the course short and have taken care to keep away the best runner. You can imagine that, the first step thus taken, it is not difficult for me to keep him in training. . This advantage is productive of another which I did not anticipate: when he won the prize but rarely, he used to eat it all, like the others; but, being accustomed to win it often, he becomes generous and lets the losers share. This circumstance furnished me with a moral observation, and I learned the true principle of generosity.

Continuing to make my little runners set out from different starting-points, I contrived, without his noticing it, that the distances should not be the same. Though I left my pupil the choice, he never knew how to take advantage of it. Without troubling himself about the distance, he always chose the smoothest ground. . . . I had the greatest trouble to make him see that I was tricking him. At last, in spite of his inattention, I gain my point; and he reproaches me for the trick. I ask him what right he has to complain. "If I give you a cake, may I not make my own terms? You are not obliged to run, and I did not promise to make the distances equal. You always have the choice: choose the shortest; no one will stop you." The point was

obvious, and he saw it. He began by stepping the
distances, but he soon found this method slow and
inaccurate . . . ; besides, he was vexed that time should
be wasted in measuring which might be spent in running
more races. So he learned to see better and to estimate
distances by the eye. In a word, some months of trial
and error so improved his range that, as soon as I put a
cake at hazard on any object, he estimated its distance
at a glance almost as well as if he had measured it with
a chain.

. . . The most penetrating sight can give us no idea
of extension apart from the touch and without a course
of movements. The universe must appear to an oyster
as a single point; it would so appear even if the oyster
had a human soul. It is only by walking, touching,
counting, and marking the dimensions of objects, that
we learn to make estimates of them; but, if we accustom
ourselves always to measure them, the sense, trusting to
the instrument, acquires no accuracy in estimating without it. A child should not pass too suddenly from
measurements to estimates; he should at first compare
by parts what he cannot compare as wholes; next he
should substitute estimated fractions for exact fractions;
and finally, instead of always measuring these by hand,
he should learn to do so by eye. I would have him,
however, confirm his estimates at first by real measurement, in order to correct his errors and, if any false
appearance still remain in the sensation, to learn to
rectify it by an improvement in his judgment.

e. Activities conducing to Training of the Senses.

We cannot judge accurately of the dimensions of
bodies, unless we learn to analyze and even to imitate,
their shapes: for drawing is based entirely on the laws

of perspective, and we cannot estimate size from appearance unless we have some knowledge of those laws. Children, being great imitators, all try to draw; my pupil will study this art, not precisely for its own sake, but to give him a good eye and a supple hand. Whatever be the subject, it matters little whether he perform any particular exercise, provided he acquires the delicacy of sense and the agility of body which that exercise is calculated to train. I shall therefore be careful not to send him to a drawing-master, who would only teach him to imitate imitations and to draw from copies. I wish him to have no other master than Nature, no other model than the objects themselves. He should have the original before his eyes, not the paper representing it; he should draw a house from a house, a tree from a tree, and a man from a man. Thus he will be accustomed accurately to observe the appearances of bodies, and not to mistake false and conventional imitations for genuine representations. I would even discourage his trying to draw from memory, till frequent observation had strongly impressed the true shape on his imagination; lest, through the substitution of strange fantastic shapes for the reality, he should lose his sense of proportion and his taste for the beauties of Nature.

I know that this method will, for a long time, lead to unrecognizable daubs; that he will be late in acquiring elegance in outline and the light touches of the draughtsman; and that he will, perhaps, never attain an eye for pictorial effect or a good taste in design. By way of recompense, he will certainly acquire a more accurate eye and a steadier hand; he will learn to know the true relations of size and shape between animals, plants, and other natural objects; and he will be quicker to detect the effects of perspective. This is the very aim which I have in view; my intention is not so much that he should imitate objects as that he should know them; I should much prefer him to be able to show me an acanthus than to be an adept in drawing the leaves on a capital.

In this exercise, as in all others, I do not intend that my pupil should have the amusement all to himself. I would make it still more agreeable to him by constantly sharing it. I wish him to have no other rival than myself. My rivalry will be without relaxation and without risk; it will make our employment interesting, but it will not excite jealousy. I shall follow his example in taking up the pencil; I shall use it at first as badly as my pupil. Though I were an Apelles, I would appear a mere dauber. My first sketches of a man will be like those which boys draw on the walls; a stroke for each arm, a stroke for each leg, and the fingers thicker than the arms. After some time one of us will notice the want of proportion; we shall remark that a man's leg has a certain thickness, that the thickness varies, that the length of the arms bears a certain proportion to the height of the body, etc. In this progress I shall keep pace with him; or advance so little ahead that he can easily overtake me, sometimes surpass me. We shall have brushes and colours; we shall try to imitate appearance and colour as well as shape. We shall colour, paint, daub; but in all our daubings we shall never cease to watch Nature, we shall do nothing save under the eye of our master.

We were some time ago in difficulties about the ornaments of our rooom; we can now supply them. I have our drawings framed and covered with glass, that they may receive no further touches, but may remain as we left them. We have thus a motive for not being careless. I arrange them in order round the room, each drawing repeated twenty or thirty times; they will thus display the progress of the artist, from the time when a house was a mere rude square, till its front and its sides, its proportions and its shades, are absolutely true to nature. These stages cannot fail to give us a constant supply of pictures, which will interest ourselves and be an object of curiosity to others; our emulation will always be excited.

Our first rude daubs will need to be set off by fine gilt frames; as the drawings improve and the imitation becomes more exact, I shall be content with plain black frames. The pictures no longer need extraneous ornament; it would be a pity if the attention due to the picture were distracted by the frame. Hence we both aspire to the honour of a plain frame; and, when either of us wishes to disparage the performance of the other, he condemns it to a gilt frame. Some day no doubt these gilt frames will pass into a proverb with us, and we shall be astonished to see how many people do themselves justice by a similar adornment of their own persons.

I have said that geometry is above the capacity of children; but it is our own fault. We do not perceive that their method is not ours; that what is for us the art of reasoning must be for them only the art of seeing. Instead of teaching them our method, we ought to study theirs; for our way of learning geometry is as much an affair of the imagination as of reasoning. When the enunciation is given, we have to *imagine* the proof, that is, we endeavour to find from what proposition already known the other is a consequence, and from all the consequences which may be drawn from such proposition, to choose the precise one which is relevant.

By this method the most exact reasoner, unless he has a gift of invention, will be brought to a standstill. And, what is the result? Instead of teaching us to find the proofs, they dictate them to us; instead of teaching the pupil to reason, the master reasons for him and exercises only his memory.

Make accurate figures, combine them, superimpose them, and examine their relations—you will find out the whole of elementary geometry in proceeding from observation to observation, without troubling yourself about definitions, problems, or any other form of proof except simple superposition. For my part, I do not intend to teach Émile geometry; he will teach me. I shall search for relations and he will find them; for I shall look for them in such a way as to make him find them. Instead of taking a pair of compasses, for example, to describe a circle, I shall do it with a piece of thread turning on a pivot. When I come to compare the length of the radii, Émile will laugh at me and explain that the same thread stretched out to the full was bound to cover equal distances. . . .

Teachers neglect accuracy in the figures; this is assumed, and the stress is laid on the proof. We on the contrary care nothing about proofs; our most important concern will be to draw our lines quite straight, quite exact, and quite equal; to make a square perfectly square and a circle perfectly round. To verify the accuracy of the figure, we shall examine it in the light of all its sensible properties; and this will give us every day an opportunity to discover new properties. We shall fold the two halves of a circle about the diameter and those of a square about the diagonal. . . . We shall discuss whether the equality thus observed obtains also in the case of the parallelogram, the trapezium, and other figures. Sometimes we shall try to forecast the result of the experiment before we make it, to give reasons, etc.

Thus geometry would be to my pupil only the art of using a ruler and compass; he should never confuse it with drawing, in which he uses neither of these instruments. Indeed they will always be kept under lock and key; and he will very seldom, and only for a short time, be allowed to use them, that he may not become slovenly in his drawing. . . .

[As drawing stands to seeing, so do speech and music to hearing. As children have no sentiment, there can be no expression in their speech or singing.]

In singing, make his voice true, equal, flexible, and resonant, and his ear sensible to measure and harmony; nothing more. Imitative and theatrical music is above his capacity. I would not have him even make use of words in singing; or, if he desired them, I should try to compose songs expressly for him, which should be adapted to a child's interest and should be as simple as his ideas.

It will be easily imagined that, as I am in no haste to teach him to read ordinary script, I shall be in no greater hurry to teach him to read music. . . . A tune is more faithfully conveyed by the ear than by the eye. Add to this, for a proper understanding of music, it is not enough to be able to render the work of others : we must learn to compose ourselves, and the two things should be taught simultaneously; otherwise we shall never be good musicians. . . .

f. Physical Activities.

When a child plays at battledore and shuttlecock, he exercises his eyes and arms; when he whips a top, he acquires strength by exerting it; but in neither case does he learn anything. I have often asked why children are not encouraged to play the same games of skill as men, such as tennis, fives, billiards, archery, and football, or to play on musical instruments. The reply has always been that some of these games are too much for their strength, and others require more developed limbs and organs. These reasons strike me as very unsatisfactory. A child has not the stature of a man, yet he wears clothes of the same shape. I do not mean that he should play billiards with a full-sized cue or at a table three feet high, or tennis in men's courts with a heavy racket. He should at first play in a room with barred windows, and use soft balls and light wooden rackets, which should later be changed for parchment, and finally for catgut, as he increases in strength. You prefer shuttlecock because it is less tiring and dangerous. In both reasons you are wrong. Shuttlecock is a woman's game. . . . Men are meant to be vigorous, and cannot become so without effort. How will they become capable of defending themselves if they are never attacked? Nothing renders the arms so active as the necessity of securing the head, or the sight so quick as that of preserving the eyes. To spring from one side of a tennis-court to the other, to judge of the rebound of a ball while it is still in the air, and to return it with a sure and steady arm—these are not so much games for the amusement of men as means to make men.

I may be told that I am falling into the same error of premature development with regard to the body which I have condemned in regard to the mind. There is a great difference; in the one case progress is only apparent, in the other it is real. . . Besides, it should be remembered that this training is or should be merely play, an easy and voluntary direction to a given purpose of move-

ments which Nature in any case requires.   It is a way of
varying children's amusements to make them more agreeable, and involves not the least restraint, such as would
turn them into work. . . .

g. Food.

[A long section.   The main points are (1) that Nature
gives us tastes in food which will conduce to self-
preservation; (2) there is little danger that gluttony
will become a habit; (3) a plea for vegetarianism, leading to a long digression; (4) a claim that the liking for
alcohol is entirely an acquired taste contrary to Nature.
A section on the sense of smell follows.]

3. ÉMILE AT THE AGE OF TWELVE.

[After a passage on the charm of childhood, he goes
on to speak of the ordinary child.]

The clock strikes; what a change ! In a moment his
eyes lose their fire, his cheerfulness is at an end.   Farewell to joy and play ! A stern crabbed man takes him
by the hand, says gravely " Come, sir " and leads him
away. The room they enter is full of books. Books!
dull furniture indeed for a child ! The poor boy lets
himself be dragged in, casts a regretful glance on everything around him, and says nothing : his eyes swim with
tears which he dares not shed, and his heart swells with
sighs which he dares not vent.

Child, who hast no such fear, always a stranger to
trouble and restraint, who seest the day come without
alarm, the night without impatience, and reckonest the
hours only by thy pleasures, come, my happy, my lovable
pupil and comfort me by thy presence for the departure
of this unfortunate. He comes; I feel at his approach
a sensation of joy, which I can see he shares. It is his

friend, his comrade, the companion of his sports, that he approaches; he is certain, whenever he sees me, that he will not be long without amusement; we are never dependent on each other, but we always agree, and are never so happy with anyone else as we are together.

His bearing, gait, and looks speak of confidence and content; his face is the picture of health; his firm step gives him an air of vigour; his complexion, delicate without being pale, has nothing in it of effeminacy; the sun and wind have already given him the honourable hue of his sex: his features, though still plump, begin to assume a distinguishing character; his eyes, not yet animated by the glow of sentiment, have all their natural serenity; they are not grown dull with long grief, nor have incessant tears made furrows in his cheeks. You see in his alert but steady movements the vivacity of his age, an assured independence, and an experience gained from varied exercises. He has a free and open mien, without the least insolence or vanity; his head, which has never bent over books, does not hang over his chest; there is no occasion to bid him keep it up; neither fear nor shame ever made him hang it down.

Put him in the midst of the assembly; examine him, ask him what questions you please; you need not fear impertinence, prattle, or indiscreet questions. You need not be afraid that he will take possession of you and claim to occupy your whole time, or that you will not be able to get rid of him.

At the same time you must not expect of him amusing conversation or a string of anecdotes which I have taught him. Only expect the bare plain truth, without ornament, without preparation, and without vanity. He will tell you his thoughts and actions, bad as well as good, without the least concern as to the effect which his words produce on you. He will use the gift of speech in all its original simplicity.

We are fond of basing indications of promise on some happy utterance which has fallen by chance from children's lips; and we are constantly pained by the succession of silly remarks which almost always upset our auguries. If my pupil seldom excites such hopes, he will never occasion such regret; for he will never utter a useless word, nor waste his breath in talk to which he knows that no-one will listen. His ideas are limited, but clear; if he knows nothing by rote, he knows much by experience. If he reads less than other children in books, he reads more in the book of Nature. His understanding does not lie on his tongue, but in his brain; his judgment is superior to his memory; he can speak only one language, but he understands what he says; and, though he may not talk so well as others, he will act much better.

He knows nothing of routine, fashion, or habit; what he did yesterday has no influence on what he does to-day. He follows no formula, is influenced by no authority or example, and acts and speaks only from his own judgment. Hence you must never expect of him second-hand speeches or studied manners, but always the faithful expression of his ideas and the conduct which springs from his inclinations.

You will find in him a few moral notions which relate to his actual condition, but none on the relations of man to man. Of what use would they be? A child is not yet an active member of the community. Talk to him of liberty, property, or even convention, he will so far understand you: he knows why some things belong to him and others do not; beyond this he knows nothing.

Speak to him of duty and obedience, he does not know what you mean. Command him, he will take no notice; but say, "If you will do me this favour, I will repay you some time," he will fly immediately to oblige you: for he desires nothing more than to extend his power, and to acquire over you claims which he knows to be inviolable. Perhaps he will not even be sorry to be recognized, to count for something, to be regarded as of some consequence; but, if he feels this motive, he has already abandoned Nature, and you have not closed in advance all the avenues to vanity.

If he has any need of help, he will ask it indifferently of the first person he meets, of a king as readily as of a footman; in his eyes all men are equal. You see by his way of asking that he thinks nothing due to him. He knows that he is asking a favour; he knows, too, that it is humanity to grant it. His words are simple and straightforward; his voice, his looks, his gestures are those of a being equally accustomed to meet with compliance and with refusal. He shows neither the mean and servile submission of a slave, nor the imperious tone of a master—but a modest confidence in his fellow-creatures, the noble and affecting complacence of a being, free, but feeble and sensitive, who desires the aid of another being, equally free, but powerful and kind. If you comply with his request, he will not thank you; but he will feel that he has contracted an obligation. If you refuse, he will not complain; he will not insist, he knows it would be useless; he will not say, "That has been refused," but, "It was impossible," and, as I have observed already, we never rebel against an acknowledged necessity.

Leave him alone and at liberty; note his actions without speaking to him; observe what he does in such a situation and how he goes about it. Having no need to convince himself of his freedom, he will do nothing out of wantonness, or merely to show his power; does he not know that he is always master of his own actions? He is alert, light, and active; his movements have all the vivacity of his years, but you will never see one without a purpose. Whatever he wishes to do, he will undertake nothing above his capacities; for he has tried them and knows them well: the means will always be suitable to his purpose, and he will rarely attempt anything without being assured of success. His eye will be attentive and accurate; he will never go about idly, asking others about what he sees; but he will examine it himself, and will take great pains to find out what he wishes to know before he asks questions. If he falls into unexpected situations, he will be less perplexed than other boys; and, if there be danger, less frightened. As his imagination remains still inactive and nothing has been done to arouse it, he only sees facts; he estimates danger at its true value; and always remains cool. He has too often been obliged to submit to necessity to think of opposing it now; he has felt its yoke from the cradle; he is well accustomed to it, and is prepared for anything.

Whether he is at work or at play, both are alike to him; his games are his business, he knows no distinction. His interest in everything he does keeps him in smiles; his liberty is his delight; his occupations show both the nature of his tastes and the limits of his knowledge. Is it not a sweet and charming sight to see a handsome boy, his eye gay and lively, his air content and happy, with an open smiling countenance, playing at the most serious occupations, or profoundly busied in the most childish amusements?

Would you now judge him by comparison? Let him

mix with other children and let him act; you will soon see which is the more truly formed, which comes nearer the perfection of their age. Among town children none is more skilful, but he is stronger than any. Among country children he is equal in strength and superior in ingenuity. In all that is within the capacity of a child, he judges, reasons, and foresees, better than all. In running, jumping, moving bodies, or lifting weights; in estimating distance, inventing games, and winning the prizes—one would imagine all nature at his command, so well does he know how to adapt everything to his wishes. He is formed to guide and to govern his equals; ingenuity and experience serve him instead of right and authority. Give him what garb and name you please, it is no matter; he will always lead, always be the head of his companions, and they will always feel his superiority. Without the wish to command, he will be master; without realizing that they obey, they will be his subjects. . . .

The great inconvenience in this early education is that the effects are visible only to the clear-sighted; to the common-eye a child who has been brought up with so much care appears only as a gutter-child. A tutor thinks more of his own interest than of his pupil's; he is trying to prove that he is not wasting his time and that he is worth a higher salary. He provides his pupil with a stock of acquisitions which are easily gained and easily displayed; he does not care whether they are useful, provided they make a display, and loads his memory with an ill-assorted heap of indiscriminate rubbish.

When the child is to be examined, he is made to exhibit his stock; he displays it, and we are satisfied. Then he packs up his bale and departs. My pupil is not so rich; he has no packet to display, nothing to exhibit but himself. A child is no more known at sight than a man. Where is the observer who can detect his characteristic features at a glance? Doubtless they exist, but they are very few; you will not find one such father among a hundred.

A multiplicity of questions tires and disgusts everyone, especially children. After a few minutes, their attention flags; they no longer listen to the inquiries of the obstinate questioner, and they answer only at random. This method of examination is futile and pedantic; often a chance word gives a better insight into their mind and character than a tedious conversation; but we must make sure that such a word is neither accidental nor second-hand. To estimate the judgment of a child needs great judgment in the observer. I remember a story related by the late Lord Hyde of a friend who, returning from Italy after three years' absence, wished to examine the progress of his son, a boy about nine or ten. One evening they took a walk with the tutor in a field where some schoolboys were amusing themselves by flying kites. The father suddenly asked, "Where is the kite that throws that shadow?" Without hesitating or raising his eyes, the boy answered, "On the road." "And in fact," added Lord Hyde, "the road was between us and the sun. . . ."

VI

EXTRACTS FROM "ÉMILE," BOOK III. (ON EDUCATION FROM TWELVE TO FIFTEEN)

1. Motives for Choice of Studies; Curiosity and Utility.

ALTHOUGH the whole period up to adolescence is one of weakness, there is a certain point at which the increase of strength has outrun present needs, and the growing animal, though absolutely weak, becomes relatively strong. . . . At twelve or thirteen years of age, the faculties of a child develop far more rapidly than his wants. . . . It is the only time in his life when this will be the case. . . .

How shall we use this transitory surplus of strength and abilities? He should employ it on such occupations as may profit him when need arises. He should, as it were, lay by his present surplus as stock-in-hand for the future. The strong child should make provision for the weak man. . . . This then is the time for work, for learning, for study. Observe that this is no arbitrary choice on my part, but is the plain intention of Nature.

Human intelligence has its bounds; we cannot know everything; indeed no one man can know completely the little which is known. . . . Selection becomes necessary among subjects, as well as among periods for learning them. Of the possible branches of study, some are false, others useless, and others calculated only to flatter the vanity of their possessors. The few which really contribute to our well-being are alone worthy of the attention of a wise man, and therefore of a child whom we wish to make such. Our aim is not knowledge, but useful knowledge.

From this scanty residue we must further subtract those which, to study them, require a mind already formed, those which involve a knowledge of human relations which a child cannot understand, and those which, though true in themselves, dispose an inexperienced mind to think wrongly on other topics. We are thus reduced to a very small circle compared with the scope of reality, but it appears an immense sphere to the limited faculties of a child. . . .

We are gradually approaching those moral ideas which discriminate good and evil. Hitherto we have known no law but necessity; now we are concerned with utility; soon we shall reach morality and propriety.

The various faculties of man are excited by the same instinct. To the activity of the body, which strives to grow, succeeds that of the mind, which strives to learn. At first children are purely motor beings, afterwards they become inquisitive; and this curiosity, well directed, becomes, at the age which we have now reached, their chief spring of action. Let us always distinguish the propensities of Nature from those of opinion. Thirst for knowledge may proceed merely from the desire to be thought clever; but there is another kind which springs from a natural curiosity concerning everything in which we may be directly or indirectly interested. Our innate desire of happiness and the impossibility of fully gratifying it are the cause of constant researches after new expedients which may contribute to that end.

Such is the original motive of curiosity, a motive truly innate, though its development is conditioned by our desires and our knowledge. Suppose a philosopher cast ashore on a desert island with his books and instruments, and sure of spending the rest of his life in that solitude. He would trouble no more about the Solar System, the law of gravitation, or the differential calculus. Perhaps he would never open a book all his life; but he would certainly not fail to explore the island, however extensive, to its remotest corners. Let us therefore further reduce our list by rejecting those studies for which man has no natural taste and confining ourselves to those which instinct leads us to pursue.

2. STUDIES BASED ON CURIOSITY.

a. Geography.

The Earth is man's island and the Sun his most striking spectacle. As soon as our ideas begin to extend beyond ourselves, our attention will necessarily be attracted to one or other of these two objects. Hence the philosophy of almost every savage nation is confined solely to the imaginary divisions of the Earth and the divinity of the Sun. "What a departure!" cries the reader. "We were but now employed on our immediate surroundings; and here we are, traversing the Earth and soaring to the bounds of the sky." This departure, reader, is the simple effect of the progress of our powers and the bent of our minds. During the period of weakness and insufficiency, the needs of self-preservation confined our thoughts within ourselves; in the period of capacity and power, the desire of extending our being carries us out of ourselves and extends our ideas to their utmost limits. As, however, the intellectual world is still unknown to us, our thoughts cannot extend further than we can see; and our comprehension enlarges only with the space which it measures.

Let us convert our sensations into ideas, but let us not fly at once from sensible to intellectual objects. It is only by the former that we can reach the latter. In the first operations of the understanding, let the senses be our only guide, the world our only book, and facts our only lessons. Children who read never think, they gain no knowledge, they learn only words.

Make your pupil attentive to natural phenomena and you will soon arouse his curiosity; but, to keep that curiosity alive, you must be in no haste to satisfy it. Put suitable questions and leave him to solve them. Let him know nothing because you have told him, but because he has discovered it himself; he must not *learn* science, but *find it out*. If once you substitute authority for argument in his mind, he will never reason; he will ever afterwards be the shuttlecock of others' opinions.

You intend to teach your boy geography, and you collect maps, spheres, and globes. What an array! Why all these representations? Why not begin by showing him the things themselves, that he may at least know what it is that you are talking about?

Walk out with him some fine evening to a convenient spot, from which an extensive horizon gives you a full view of the setting sun, and notice any objects which mark its setting-point. Return the next morning to take the fresh air before sunrise. His appearance is heralded by the fiery rays which he scatters before him. The brightness increases, the east seems all in flames

and you expect the glorious orb long before he appears; you think you see him every moment; at length he rises.
. . Full of the enthusiasm which he feels, a tutor wishes to communicate it to his pupil. . . . Vain hope! It is only in the heart of man that the beauties of Nature live: to be seen they must be felt. A child sees the objects, but cannot see the connexions which bind them together; he cannot hear the sweet harmony of their concert. It needs experience which he has not attained and sentiments which he has never felt to realize that complex impression which results from all these sensations at once. If he has never travelled over arid deserts, if burning sands have never parched his feet, if he never has felt the scorching sunbeams reflected from surrounding rocks, how can he enjoy the fresh air of a fine morning? . . .

Content yourself with presenting the right object at the right time and, when you have sufficiently excited his curiosity, ask some laconic question which will put him in the way of satisfying it. In this case, having carefully watched the rising Sun and made your pupil notice hills and other neighbouring objects, allow him to talk about them quite informally. Stand still a few moments as if day-dreaming, and then address him thus: "I am thinking that the Sun set last night over there, and this morning he is risen here. How can that be?" Say no more; and, if he asks questions, do not answer, but talk of something else. Leave him to himself, and be sure he will think about it.

To accustom a child to be attentive and to be really impressed by visible phenomena, he must be kept some days in suspense before discovering the explanation. If he does not understand the present problem by the means proposed, it may be made more obvious to sense-perception by varying its form. If he cannot understand how the Sun proceeds from its setting to its rising, he knows at least how it proceeds from its rising to its setting; his eyes teach him this. Explain the first problem by the second; and if your pupil be not extremely dull, the analogy is too obvious to escape him. Such is our first lesson in astronomy.

Since we proceed slowly from one sensible idea to another, familiarizing ourselves for a long time with each before we pass to the next, and since our pupil's attention is never forced, it will be a long journey from this first lesson to the knowledge of the Sun's course and of the shape of the Earth: but as the apparent motion of all the heavenly bodies depends on the same principle, and the first observation leads to all the rest, it requires less effort, though more time, to proceed from the daily rotation of the Earth to the calculation of an eclipse than is needed to acquire clear ideas of day and night. . . .

We have seen the Sun rise at midsummer: we shall now watch his rising at Christmas, or on some fine winter morning. We are neither of us idle, and both despise the cold. I take care to make the second observation on the same spot as before and to prepare the way by a little conversation, so that one or other of us is bound to cry out, "How strange! the Sun is not rising in the same place. There are our old landmarks, and now he rises yonder! So there is a summer east and a winter east!"

These examples will suffice to show how you can teach the "Use of the Globes" very clearly from the real objects. It may be laid down as a general rule never to substitute the representation for the reality, except when it is impossible to exhibit the latter; the representation engrosses the child's attention and makes him forget the reality.

[He then shows the faults of the armillary sphere.]

We never know how to put ourselves in the place of children; we never enter into their manner of thinking, but attribute to them our own ideas. Always following our own method of argument, we contrive even with chains of truths only to fill their heads with misunderstandings and mistakes. It is disputed whether science is best taught analytically or synthetically. It is not necessary always to keep to one of these methods. We may sometimes combine and analyze in the same investigation, and lead a child by the didactic method while he himself believes that he is only analyzing. Further, if we employ both methods indifferently, they serve to confirm one another. Setting out at the same time from two different points, without thinking that he is making for the same spot, he will be surprised to find the two routes meeting; and the surprise cannot fail to give him great satisfaction. I would, for example, begin geography at the two extremes and unite with the study of the Earth's motions the measurement of its parts, beginning in his own locality. While he is studying the sphere and transporting himself to the sky, call him back to the divisions of the Earth and show him first his own home.

His two topographical starting-points will be the town where he lives and his father's country house; then follow intermediate places, next the neighbouring rivers, and finally the direction of the Sun and the method of finding the points of the compass. This is the point of reunion. Let him make a map of it all, beginning simply with the two starting-points, and inserting the rest by degrees as he discovers or estimates their position and distance. You now see the advantage which he has already secured by carrying his compass in his eyes.

Notwithstanding this advantage, it will be necessary to guide him a little, but very little and without his knowing it. If he makes mistakes, let him. Do not correct them; wait till he is in a position to discover and correct them himself; or at most on some favourable opportunity suggest some piece of work which will reveal them to him. If he never makes mistakes, he will not learn so well. Our object is not that he should know the exact topography of the country but the means of discovering it; it is of no importance to him to have a number of maps in his head, provided he knows what they represent and has a clear idea of the method of constructing them. Here you see the difference between Émile's ignorance and other boys' knowledge. They know maps, he makes them. Here are new ornaments for our room.

b. Physical Science.

Always remember that the spirit of my instruction is not to teach a child many things, but to allow only true and clear ideas to enter his mind. His knowing little is of no consequence if he is not deceived. I store his head with truths only to keep out the errors which he would learn in their place. Reason and judgment advance slowly, prejudices assail him in crowds; it is from the latter that we must carefully guard him. If you value knowledge for its own sake, you enter upon an unfathomable boundless ocean, full of rocks; you will never escape from it. When I see a man, stricken with the love of knowledge, letting himself be led astray by its charms, and flying from one science to another, unable to stop his course, I think of a child gathering shells on the shore.

He gathers a first load ; then, tempted by others, he throws the first away ; and so he goes on, picking up and casting aside, till, bewildered by their number, he ends by throwing all away and returns home empty.

During the first period, time was long and we tried only to lose it, for fear we might use it badly. The case is now altered; we have not enough to do all that might be useful. The passions advance apace and, the moment they knock at the gate, your pupil will give no ear to ought else. The term of dispassionate intelligence is so short and transitory, and has so many other necessary uses, that it is folly to think it long enough to make a child learned. It is not our aim to teach him the sciences, but to give him a taste to love them and a method by which to learn them when this taste is better developed. This is a fundamental principle of all rational education.

This is also the time gradually to accustom your pupil to give sustained attention to one object. This attention, however, must always be aroused by pleasure or inclination, never by constraint. We must also be careful that it does not overburden him and pass into boredom. Keep a careful watch and, whatever happens, stop before he is tired. He had better learn nothing than learn upon compulsion.

If he asks a question, let your answers be calculated to keep alive his curiosity rather than to satisfy it, especially when you observe that he is not seeking information but is talking at random and wearying you with silly questions. You should pay less regard to the actual words than to his motives for inquiry. This treatment becomes of the greatest importance when a child begins to reason.

There is a chain of general truths by which all the

sciences are dependent on certain common principles and may be successively deduced from them. This sequence constitutes the method of men of science: we are not considering it here. There is another sequence by which every particular object brings some other in its train and always points to that which follows it. This order, which keeps alive our attention by a continual curiosity, is followed by a majority of adults and is peculiarly adapted to children. . . .

[The juggler incident which follows is much condensed.]

One day we go to the fair; a juggler is attracting a wax duck with a piece of bread. On our return home, it occurs to us to imitate it. We take a large needle and, after touching it on the loadstone, we cover it with wax, which we mould as well as we can into the shape of a duck. We set it afloat in a basin and, presenting a key to its beak, find to our joy that the duck follows it. In the evening we return to the fair with a piece of bread properly prepared in our pocket; as soon as the juggler has performed his trick, my young scientist, with difficulty containing himself, tells him that it is quite easy and that he can do it as well himself. He is taken at his word. [The trick succeeds;] the juggler, though a little confounded, embraces him, congratulates him, and begs him to honour him with his presence the next day, when he promises to collect a larger audience to admire his skill. [He goes; there is a large audience; his turn comes.] He approaches, a trifle abashed; he offers his bread to the duck—what a change of fortune! The duck, so tame yesterday, has turned wild to-day. Instead of presenting its beak, it turns tail and swims away. At last Émile retires in confusion. unable to bear the hisses of the company. The next morning there is a knock at the door: I open it and find the juggler. He modestly complains of our conduct; he cannot think what he has done to us that we should try to discredit his tricks and deprive him of his bread. "Nevertheless, gentlemen, I am ready to explain the secret that so much embarrassed you, but I beg you not to use it to my prejudice." He produces his apparatus, when to our great surprise we see that it consists only of a powerful magnet, manipulated by a boy who is concealed under the table. How many lessons are contained in this single one! How many mortifying consequences are sure to follow the first emotion of vanity! Watch carefully this first emotion in your pupil, and be sure that, if you can thus make it productive of humiliation and disgrace, it will be long before the occurrence of a second!

[They now apply the compass to discover direction.]

There are various climates on the Earth and different temperatures in those climates. The seasons vary more considerably as we approach the poles. Bodies contract with cold and expand with heat; this effect is most conspicuous in liquids and specially in spirituous liquids; hence the thermometer. The wind strikes our faces; therefore the air is a body, a fluid, which we feel, though we cannot see it. Invert a glass in water, the water will not fill it unless you let the air escape: air is therefore capable of resistance. Lower the glass, and the water will gain on the air, though not entirely filling the glass; therefore up to a certain point air is compressible. A ball filled with compressed air rebounds better than one filled with any other substance; air is therefore elastic. Lying at full length in your bath, raise your arm horizontally out of the water; you will find it loaded with an enormous weight; air therefore has weight. This weight may be ascertained by balancing air against other fluids; hence the barometer, the syphon, the air-gun, and the air-pump. All the laws of statics and dynamics can be discovered by equally simple experiments. I would not have Émile enter a laboratory to learn any of them. The scientific air kills science. These instruments either frighten a child or attract to their form the attention which he ought to bestow on their effects. I prefer that we should make our apparatus ourselves. I would not begin by constructing the instrument before the experiment; but, having met with a suggestion of the experiment as it were by chance, we would by degrees invent the instrument which is needed to confirm our surmise. I prefer that our instruments should be less accurate and complete, but that we should have clearer ideas of what they ought to be and of the operations which should result from them. For my first lesson in statics, instead of providing myself with a balance, I lay a stick across the back of a chair; I measure the length of the two parts in equilibrium; I hang on each side weights, sometimes equal, sometimes unequal, pushing the stick one way or the other as occasion requires, till I find that equilibrium results from a reciprocal proportion between the weight of the bodies and the length of the levers; and thus I instruct my young mechanic to rectify a balance before he has ever seen one.

We acquire without doubt clearer and more certain notions of things which we thus learn for ourselves than of those which we are taught by others. Further, instead of accustoming our reason to a servile acceptance of authority, we grow more ingenious in discovering relations, in connecting our ideas, and in inventing instruments; whereas, by adopting those which are given us, we let our mind grow dull and indifferent, like the man who is dressed by valets, served by attendants, and drawn by horses, till he loses by degrees the free use of his limbs. . . .

The most obvious advantage of these slow and laborious researches is to preserve, in the midst of speculative studies, the activity of the body and the suppleness of the limbs; to train the hands to work and accustom them to such habits as are of use to mankind. So many instruments, invented to direct us in our experiments and to supply the deficiencies of our senses, make us neglect their exercise. A theodolite saves us from estimating the size of angles; the eye, which can measure distances with precision, gives up the task to the chain; the steelyard excuses me from judging weight by hand. The more ingenious our instruments, the more dull and incapable become our organs; by collecting machines about us, we lose those that are within us.

But, when we use for the construction of these instruments the skill which would take their place, we gain without losing anything; we add art to nature and become more ingenious without being less dexterous. If, instead of keeping a boy poring over books, I employ him in a workshop, his hands will be busied to the improvement of his understanding; he will become a philosopher, while he thinks himself only an artisan. . . .

I have remarked that purely speculative knowledge is not suited to children, even when they approach adolescence; still, without entering too early into systematic physics, you should secure that all their experiments are connected by some species of deduction: by aid of this sequence they will be able to arrange them in an orderly manner in their minds, and to recall them when needed.

It is very difficult to retain isolated facts or even arguments long in the memory without some clue for their recall.

3. STUDIES BASED ON UTILITY.

a. General Principles.

As soon as a child acquires enough knowledge of himself to realize in what his happiness consists, as soon as his knowledge of relations becomes sufficiently extensive to discriminate what is good for him and what is not, he is in a position to distinguish work from play, and to regard the latter only as a relaxation from the former. Objects of real use may then enter into his studies, and may claim a more sustained attention than he would give to mere amusements. The ever recurring law of necessity teaches us at an early stage to perform unpleasant tasks in order to avoid still more unpleasant consequences.

When boys foresee their wants before they arise, their understanding is considerably advanced, and they begin to realize the value of time. They should therefore be accustomed to employ it to useful purpose; but the purpose should be such as they can understand and within the reach of their capacities. We should avoid anything which arises out of the moral order or out of the customs of society; for they are not yet capable of understanding such matters. It is folly to require them to devote themselves to pursuits which they are vaguely told are for their good, while they are ignorant in what that good consists. It is useless to assure them that they will find these occupations useful in later life or to expect any present interest in an alleged advantage which they cannot understand. . . .

" What is the use of this ?" Henceforward this is the

consecrated and decisive formula between us on all occasions. It is the question with which I shall infallibly meet all his inquiries : it will serve as a check to those silly and troublesome questions with which children are always teasing their elders, more for the sake of exercising a kind of domination than from a desire of information. What a powerful instrument have I here put into your hands for the conduct of your pupil ! Not knowing a reason for anything, he is reduced to silence whenever you please ; while, on the other hand, what an advantage your knowledge and experience give you in proving the utility of whatever you propose ! . . .

Let us suppose that, while I am studying with my pupil the course of the Sun and the method of finding direction, he should stop me by asking to what purpose is all this. I might talk to him of the utility of travelling, the advantages of commerce. . . . When I had done, I should only have been exposing my own pedantry ; my pupil would not have understood a word. . . . I propose a walk before breakfast ; he likes nothing better ; we enter the forest, lose ourselves, and cannot find our way out. Time presses ; the heat increases ; we are hungry ; we grow flurried, we wander aimlessly from place to place ; we see nothing but trees, quarries, and glades. We sit down to rest and think. [After various preliminary matter, the tutor remarks :] " It is noon, the exact time when we were here yesterday, noticing the position of the forest from Montmorency : if only we could observe the position of Montmorency from the forest !" " Yes ! but yesterday we saw the forest, and here we can't see the town." " That's the pity. If only we could find out its position without seeing it !" " Oh, sir ?" " Did we not say that the forest was——" " To the north of Montmorency." " So Montmorency must be——" "To the south of the forest." "We know how to find the north at noon." "Yes, by the shadows." "And the south?" "How shall we find that?" "The south is opposite the north." "Yes; we've only to go the other way to our shadows; that's south. Montmorency must be that side; let's look." "You may be right; let's take this path through the wood." Émile, clapping his hands and shouting for joy, "Ah! I see Montmorency straight in front of us quite clearly. Come along! let's go to breakfast—to dinner; let's make haste : astronomy, I see, is some use."

[Another anecdote follows about some adulterated wine.]

b. Robinson Crusoe.

I hate books; they only teach people to talk about things which they do not understand. It is said that Hermes engraved the elements of the sciences on columns, to secure his discoveries from being lost in the flood. Had he imprinted them on the minds of men, they would have been preserved by tradition. . . . Is there no means of collecting the lessons which are scattered up and down so many volumes? of uniting them under a common purpose which may be easily understood, may be followed with interest, and may prove stimulating even to a boy? If one could only invent a situation in which all men's natural wants were shown in a form suited to the mind of a child, if the means of satisfying these wants were one by one described in the same easy manner, the simple and lively description of such a state might well be the first material for the exercise of his youthful imagination.

I see the imagination of the philosopher already take fire. Give yourself no trouble; such a situation has already been discovered; it has been described, and, I may say without any injustice, much better than you could describe it yourself, at least with more exactitude and simplicity. Since we must have books, there is one which, in my opinion, affords a complete textbook of natural education. This is the first book which Émile shall read; it will for some time compose his library, and it will always hold a distinguished place there. It will afford us the text to which all our conversations on natural science will serve only as a comment. It will provide us during our progress with a text of our judgment; and, unless our taste be vitiated, its pages will give us constant pleasure. What is this wonderful book? Is it Aristotle? Is it Pliny? Is it Buffon? No : it is Robinson Crusoe.

Robinson Crusoe on his island, deprived of the help of his fellow-men and the instruments of the arts, yet providing for his subsistence and self-preservation, and even procuring a kind of happiness—there is an object of interest to persons of every age, and there are a thousand ways of making it agreeable to children. Thus we have realized the desert island which I used at first only by way of comparison. It is not, I admit, the condition of civilized men; probably it will never be that of Émile; but it is by such a state that he ought to estimate others. The most sure means of rising superior to prejudice and of basing his judgments on the actual relations of things, is to assume the character of such an isolated being, and to judge of everything, as a man in such circumstances would, by its real utility. This romance, beginning with the shipwreck on the island and ending with the arrival of the vessel that brought him away, would, if cleared of extraneous matter, constitute at once his instruction and his amusement during the period which we are now considering. I would have his head turned by the tale. Let him be entirely taken up with his castle, his goats, and his plantations; let him learn in detail, not from books but from things, all that a man in such a situation would be bound to know. Let him think he is Crusoe himself. Let him wear a coat of skins, a large hat, an enormous sabre, and all the grotesque costume of his hero, even to his umbrella, of which he will have no need. I would have him consider what measures to take if this or that were lacking, examine his hero's conduct, and see that he had omitted nothing, and that nothing could be done in a better way. I would have him attentively notice Crusoe's mistakes and profit by avoiding them himself. . . . What opportunities does such a pretence afford to an able tutor who has encouraged it only with a view to utilizing it! The pupil, eager to furnish a store for his island, would be more ready to learn than his tutor to teach.

c. Economic Teaching.

Your greatest care should be to keep from your pupil the knowledge of those social relations which are beyond his grasp ; but, when the connexion of his ideas obliges you to speak of the mutual dependence of mankind, instead of presenting it from the moral side, divert his attention at first towards industry and the mechanical arts, which make men of use to one another. In taking him from workshop to workshop, never let him see any task performed without lending a hand, nor come out of the shop without perfectly understanding the reason of all that is being done or at least of all which he notices. To this end you should work yourself, and in every way set him the example. To make him a master.

you must be in everything an apprentice; and reflect that he will learn more by one hour of manual work than he would retain from a whole day's explanations.

The different arts are commonly valued in inverse ratio to their real use. . . . What will become of your pupil if you permit or encourage him to adopt this foolish prejudice, if for example you enter a jeweller's shop with more respect than that of a locksmith? What idea will he form of the real merit of the arts and of the intrinsic worth of commodities if he sees capricious values universally opposed to those which are based on real utility, and finds that the more a thing costs the less it is worth?

But you will say, "My son is formed to live in the world, to reside not among philosophers, but with fools; he must know their follies, since it is by their follies that they consent to be led. The knowledge of things as they are may be useful; but that of men and their opinions is much more so; for, in society, man's greatest instrument is man, and the wisest is he who can best use that instrument for his ends. To what purpose then is it to give children ideas of an imaginary order, quite contrary to that which they will find established and by which they must regulate their behaviour? First give them lessons to make them wise and then show them in what respects others are fools."

Before you tell a child about men's opinions, teach him what value to set upon them. Does he *know* folly when he regards it as wisdom? To attain wisdom, he must discern its opposite. How will your boy know mankind if he cannot pass judgment on their opinions or detect their mistakes? It is a misfortune for him to know their opinions while he is ignorant whether they are true or false. Teach him therefore what things are in themselves. . . .

It is by their obvious relations to his own convenience, security, preservation, and happiness that he should estimate all the forces of Nature and all the works of man. Hence he regards iron as far more precious than gold and glass than diamonds. For the same reason he has far more respect for a shoemaker or a mason than for all the jewellers in Europe. A pastry-cook is a person of singular importance in his eyes, and he would give the whole Academy of Science for the meanest confectioner. Goldsmiths, engravers, gilders, and embroiderers appear to him as triflers who amuse themselves in perfectly useless employment; he does not even hold a watchmaker in very high esteem. . . .

There is another order, no less natural, and still more logical; we can arrange the arts according to the necessary connexions which bind them together, placing the most independent in the first class and those which depend on the greatest number of others in the last. . . . The first of all arts and the most to be respected is agriculture; next to the farmer I rank the smith; to the smith succeeds the carpenter, and so on. A child who has not been led astray by prejudices will rank them precisely in this order. How many important reflexions on this subject will Émile draw from Robinson Crusoe! What will he think when he sees that the arts are only brought to perfection by indefinite subdivision and by multiplication of implements! He will say, "What foolish ingenuity! These people are afraid that their arms and fingers are not fit for use, so many expedients do they contrive for doing without them! To exercise a single trade, they must be assisted by a thousand others; it needs a whole town for a single worker. . . ."

Do not look merely at the bodily exercise and manual dexterity of my pupil; but consider the direction which we give to his childish curiosity; notice his good sense, his power of invention, and his foresight. Whatever he sees or does, he wants to know everything and to know the reason for everything; he traces back one instrument from another, till he reaches the first; he takes nothing on trust; he refuses to learn anything which presumes a previous knowledge which he does not possess. If he sees a spring, he wants to know how the metal was extracted from the ore. If he sees the sides of a chest fitted together, he will want to know how the tree was felled. If he is at work himself, with every new tool he uses, he never fails to say, "If I had not this tool, how shall I proceed to make one like it or to do without it?"

The child should choose his own occupations; but you should always be at his side, to observe him continually and to watch his movements without his knowing it; you should anticipate all his opinions and prevent those that are wrong; you should keep him so employed that he not only feels that he is making himself useful but is delighted at knowing the exact use of what he is doing. . . .

[This leads up to an explanation of the use of money.]

The use of this invention, thus explained, will be obvious to the dullest child. It is difficult to make a direct comparison between commodities of different kinds, for example between cloth and grain: but when a common standard such as money is established, it is easy for the manufacturer and the farmer to reduce to this standard the value of the articles which they wish to exchange. . . . Go no further than this; do not attempt to explain the moral effects of the institution.   The uses of everything should be well understood before you point out the abuses. . . .

We go to dine at the house of a wealthy family; we find elaborate preparations, a large company, a number of servants, a variety of dishes, and superb plate.   Here is something intoxicating, to those who are unused to it, in this appearance of splendour and festivity.   I foresee its effect on my young pupil.   While the repast is prolonged course after course, while brilliant conversations are going on all round the table, I whisper in his ear, " Through how many hands should you think has all we see on the table passed before it came here ?"   What a crowd of ideas will those few words bring thronging into his mind !   In an instant his delirium vanishes.   He muses, reflects, calculates, and is uneasy. . . .   The comparison between such a splendid and formal repast and a plain homely dinner, provided by his own labour and seasoned by hunger, liberty, and gaiety, is enough to make him feel that all this elaborate festivity is of no real use and that, his hunger being as fully satisfied at the table of the peasant as at that of the millionaire, he enjoys nothing more at the one than at the other which he can truly call his own.

[Then follows a long speech which the tutor must *not* make.   He then discusses the economic basis of society in the exchange of commodities.]

d. Teaching a Trade.

As soon as Émile knows what life is, my first care shall be to teach him to preserve it.   Hitherto I have made no distinction of situation, rank, or fortune, nor shall I distinguish them otherwise in the sequel; for man is the same in every rank and situation. . . . Adapt the education of man to man and not to his accidents. Do you not see that, by bringing him up to fill only one station, you unfit him for all others, and that through the caprices of fortune your pains may serve only to make him unhappy? Is there a being more ridiculous than a lord become a beggar and retaining in his misery the prejudices of his birth? . . You trust to the present order, forgetting that it is subject to unavoidable revolutions and that you can neither foresee nor prevent what may affect your children. The high becomes low, the rich poor, the monarch a subject. Are these changes of fortune so rare that you can be sure of being exempt? We are approaching a period of crisis, an age of revolutions. Who can assure you what will be your lot? All that men have made they may destroy. There are no characters indelible but those imprinted by Nature, and Nature made no man royal, noble, or rich. . . The man who consumes at leisure what he has not earned is a thief; and a pensioner, who is paid by the State for doing nothing, differs little in my eyes from a brigand, who lives by plunder on the highway. Out of society, the isolated individual, with duties to no-one, may live as he pleases: but in society, where he necessarily lives at the expense of others, he owes them the equivalent of his maintenance in the form of work, and this without exception. To work is the indispensable duty of social man. Rich or poor, strong or weak, every idle citizen is a knave.

Of all the occupations which furnish subsistence to mankind, that which approaches nearest to a state of nature is manual work: of all conditions of life, the most independent of fortune and man's caprice is that of the artisan. . . . I have no need to bid Émile learn agriculture; he knows it already. Every rustic employment is familiar to him; it was his first study, and he returns to it incessantly. I say to him therefore, "Till the inheritance of your fathers. But, if you lose that heritage, or never had one, what must you do? (Learn a trade. . . .")

The letter killeth, the spirit maketh alive. I would have him learn a trade less for its own sake than to overcome the prejudices which despise it. You will never be reduced, you say, to work for your bread. So much the worse for you; I say, so much the worse. But no matter; if you do not work from necessity, work for glory. (Stoop to the station of an artisan that you may rise above your own.) To make fortune subservient to your will, you must begin by rendering yourself independent of her. . .

Remember, it is not a hobby I ask, but a trade, a real trade, a mechanical art, in which the hands work more than the head; an art which will never bring you a fortune, but will enable you to live without it.

([Success in the professions is won by influence.])

I am determined that Émile shall learn a trade. A creditable one at least! you will say. I should like to know the meaning of the word. Is not every employment creditable that is useful to the community? I would not have him an embroiderer, a gilder, or a varnisher, like Locke's gentleman: I would have him neither a musician, an actor, nor a writer. Except these occupations and others like them, he may choose what he will. . . .

By passing before a child's eyes the products of Nature and of Art, by exciting his curiosity and tracing its tendency, we are enabled to study his tastes, inclinations, and propensities; to discover the first spark of his genius, if he have any particular bent. But it is a common mistake, against which you must carefully guard, to attribute to the warmth of genius what is merely the effect of opportunity. . . . One youth hears a drum and believes himself a general; another sees a house built and wishes to be an architect. . . .

But perhaps we are attaching undue weight to the choice of a trade. As it is only a question of handicraft, Émile need not hesitate; he has already served half his apprenticeship in the exercises to which he has been accustomed. He is ready to turn his hand to whatever you may require; he can handle spade and hoe, mallet, plane, and file; the tools of all handicrafts are familiar to him. He only needs to acquire enough skill and readiness in the use of some one of these tools to be as competent as a good workman in that particular trade. He has an agile body and supple limbs; he can throw himself into any attitude, and continue any movement for a long time without tiring. Add to this that his senses are accurate and well-trained, and that all the technique of the arts is already known to him. To turn out the work of a master, he needs nothing but practice; and practice is to be gained only by time. . . .

Let every man choose a trade befitting his sex and every young man a trade suited to his age. A close and sedentary occupation which enervates the body will neither please him nor be suitable to him. No young man will ever of his own accord aspire to be a tailor. . . . All things considered, the trade I should most desire my pupil to choose would be that of a joiner. It is neat and useful; it may be carried on indoors; it keeps the body in sufficient exercise, and requires diligence and dexterity; and, though the nature of the work is determined on grounds of utility, taste and elegance are not excluded in the execution.

If by chance your pupil's abilities are definitely turned towards the speculative sciences, I should not blame you for teaching him a trade conformable to his tastes; let him learn, for example, to make mathematical instruments—quadrants, telescopes, and the like.

When Émile learns a trade, I shall learn it with him; for I am convinced that he will never learn well what we do not learn together. We will therefore both serve an apprenticeship; not affecting to be treated as gentlemen, but as real apprentices, who are not trifling with the trade. Why should we not be so in earnest? Czar Peter served as a ship's carpenter in the yard and as a drummer to his own troops.

Unfortunately we cannot spend all our time at the bench; we are not only apprenticed joiners but men; the latter apprenticeship is much the longer and more difficult. What, then, shall we do? Shall we hire a master joiner for an hour a day as we do a dancing-master? No: we should not be his apprentices but his pupils; and our ambition is not so much to learn the trade as to raise ourselves to the condition of a joiner. I think therefore that we should go once or twice a week at least and spend the whole day at the shop; that we should rise at his hour in the morning, that we should be at our work before him, that we should eat at his table, work under his orders, and, having had the honour of supping with his family, return, if we pleased, to sleep on our own hard beds.

[He must have none of the airs of a virtuoso.]

If I have made myself understood, the reader will perceive that, by accustoming my pupil to bodily exercise and manual work, I insensibly give him a taste for reflexion and meditation, and thereby counteract the indolence which would naturally result from his indifference for the opinions of mankind and from the tranquillity of his passions. He must work like a peasant and think like a philosopher, if he is not to become as idle as a savage. The great secret of education is always to make mental and bodily exercise serve as a relaxation to each other.

4. RESULTS OF THIS PERIOD.

a. Psychology of Ideas.

Our pupil had at first only sensations; now he has ideas; once he only perceived, now he judges. It is from the comparison of several successive or simultaneous sensations and from the judgments formed thereon that there arises that kind of complex or mixed sensation which I call an idea. Minds are distinguished by the manner in which they form ideas. The deep mind forms its ideas entirely from real relations; the superficial is content with apparent relations: the accurate mind sees relations as they really are, the inaccurate misjudges them. The mind of a madman sees imaginary relations that have neither reality nor appearance; that of an idiot makes no comparisons. The greater or smaller power of comparing ideas and discovering relations constitutes a greater or smaller mind.

Simple ideas are only compared sensations. There are judgments in simple sensations as well as in complex sensations; the latter I call ideas. In sensations the judgment is merely passive; it affirms that it experiences what it experiences. But in the perception or idea, the judgment is active; it collects, compares, and determines the relations which the senses fail to determine. This is all the difference, but it is very considerable. Nature never deceives us; it is always we who deceive ourselves.

A child of eight is given an ice. He puts his spoon to his mouth, not knowing what it is; and, pained by the cold, he cries out "It burns." He feels an acute sensation, and, knowing none more acute than heat, he imagines that to be the cause. Yet he is wrong; the sudden cold may hurt, but does not burn him; nor are the two sensations alike; those who are accustomed to both never confuse them. It is not the sensation therefore that deceives him, but the judgment which he forms of it.

[The apparent movement of the moon to meet a cloud, the refraction of a stick in water, and other sensory illusions, are mentioned.]

Since all our mistakes arise from judgment, it is clear that, if we had no need to judge, we should have no occasion to learn; we should never be liable to make mistakes and should be much happier in our ignorance than we can be in our knowledge. We do not deny that the learned know a thousand truths which the ignorant will never know. Are the learned therefore nearer truth? Quite the contrary; the more they progress, the further off they are. The craving for inference outstrips their power, so that every truth which they learn brings a hundred errors in its train. Nothing is clearer than that the learned societies of Europe are schools of falsehood, that more errors are to be found in the Academy of Science than in the whole tribe of the Hurons.

Since errors increase with knowledge, ignorance is the only means of avoiding them. "What importance is it?" is the phrase most familiar among the ignorant and most needed by the learned. Unhappily this phrase is useless nowadays. Everything is important, because we are dependent on everything; and our curiosity necessarily extends with our desires. . . . Will it be said that I am deviating from Nature? I deny it. Nature, it is true, chooses her instruments, and regulates them in accordance, not with opinion, but with our necessities. But our necessities vary with our situations. There is a vast difference between the natural man in a state of solitude and the natural man in a state of society. Émile is not a savage destined to prowl in the woods, but a savage made to inhabit cities. He must know how to earn his living, to use his fellow-citizens to his advantage, and to live, if not like them, at least among them. Since amid so many new relations on which he is dependent he must perforce form judgments, let us teach him to form them correctly.

The best way to train the judgment is that which tends most to simplify our experience and even to enable us to dispense with it without falling into error. Hence it follows that, after long practice in confirming the evidence of one sense by another, we should further learn to verify the testimony of each sense by itself; every sensation will then become an idea, and that idea will always correspond with fact. Such is the kind of power which I have tried to train during this third stage.

The procedure, I own, needs a degree of patience and caution of which few tutors are capable, and without which the pupil will never learn to form correct judgments. If, for example, when he is deceived by the appearance of the stick, you are in a hurry to convince him of his mistake by taking it out of the water, you may undeceive him, but what will you teach him ? . . . To teach him better you must not correct him so soon. . . . We should (1) walk round the stick and see the apparent bend turn with us ; . . . (2) look down it from end to end, when we should not see it crooked ; . . . (3) stir the surface of the water, when we see the stick bend in various places, move zigzag, and follow the motions of the water ; . . . (4) pour out the water, when we see the stick gradually straighten as the water sinks. . . . It is not true therefore that the sight deceives us since we have no need to use any sense to rectify the errors which we attribute to it. . . .

You will tell me that this experiment involves not merely judgment, but formal reasoning. True ; but do you not see plainly that, as soon as the mind attains ideas, every judgment is a case of reasoning ? The consciousness of every sensation is a proposition, a judgment ; and as soon as we compare one sensation with another, we reason. The arts of judgment and reasoning are one and the same. . . .

b. Émile at Fifteen.

Obliged to learn for himself, he uses his own reason and not that of others ; for, if he is to give no weight to opinion, he must give none to authority ; and most of our mistakes come, not from ourselves, but from others. From this continuous exercise must result a vigour of mind, like that which is gained by the body from work and fatigue. Another advantage is that we advance only in proportion to our capacity. The mind may be overburdened as well as the body. But when the mind fully digests its acquisitions before committing them to the memory, whatever it draws from that source after-wards is properly its own. Whereas, in overcharging the memory with undigested ideas, we are in danger of never recollecting anything that can properly be called our own.

Émile has little knowledge, but what he has is truly his own; he knows nothing by halves. Among the few things he knows and knows thoroughly, the most important is that there are many things, of which he is now ignorant, which he may one day know; that there are many more known to others which he will never know; and that there is an infinity of others which no one will ever know. He has an all-round training, not in point of actual knowledge, but in the faculties of acquiring it; an open intelligent outlook, adapted to everything, and, as Montaigne says, if not instructed, at least capable of receiving instruction. It is sufficient for me that he knows how to discover the purpose of his actions and the reason for his opinions. Once again I say, my object is not to furnish his mind with knowledge, but to teach him the method of acquiring it when neces-sary, to lead him to know its exact value, and to inspire him above all with a love of truth. By this method we make small progress, but we never take a useless step and are never obliged to turn back.

Émile has no knowledge but what is merely physical. He does not even know the name of history, nor what is meant by metaphysics and ethics. He understands the essential relations between men and things, but not the moral relations between man and man. His power of generalizing and forming abstract notions is small; he observes the qualities which are common to certain bodies without reasoning on the qualities themselves. He can conceive abstract space by the help of geometrical figures and abstract quantity by means of algebraical symbols. Those figures and symbols, however, are the support of abstractions on which his senses rest. He does not try to study things by their nature, but only by relations which concern him. He estimates everything external by its relation to himself, but this estimate is accurate and steady. Caprice and custom count for nothing. He values most what is most useful; and, never varying from this standard, pays no heed to opinion.

Émile is industrious, temperate, patient, resolute, and brave. His imagination, never awakened, never exaggerates danger; he is susceptible to few evils, and knows how to bear them patiently, because he has never learned to struggle against destiny. He hardly knows the meaning of death; but, accustomed to yield to necessity without resistance, he will die when his turn comes without a murmur or complaint. This is the most our nature permits in that dreadful moment. To live independent and but little attached to human interests is the best way to learn to die.

In short, Émile is virtuous in everything relating to himself. To possess the social virtues also, he only needs to learn the relations which require them; he only wants information which his mind is ready to receive.

He thinks without regard to others and has different ideas from theirs as to what is good for him. He demands nothing from others and is aware of no obligations to others. He stands alone in the midst of society; he counts only on himself. Indeed he has a better right to do so than others; for he is all that is possible at his age. He is subject to no errors, or only to those which are inevitable; he has no vices, or only those against which no one can guard. He has a healthy constitution, agile limbs, an accurate and unprejudiced mind, and a heart free and without passions. Self-love, the first and most natural of them all, is as yet hardly aroused. Without disturbing the peace of others, he has lived as contented, happy, and free as Nature allowed. Do you think that a youth, whose character is such at fifteen, has wasted the preceding years?

VII

EXTRACTS FROM ÉMILE, BOOK IV. (ON EDUCATION AFTER FIFTEEN)

[This is the longest of the five books, but about two-fifths is occupied by a digression, "The Savoyard Curate's Confession," virtually a separate work containing Rousseau's religious views, which were those of Deism, a belief in God and a future life without any of the distinctive doctrines of Christianity.]

1. Training of the Emotions and Sentiments.

a. Psychological theory; *amour de soi* and *amour-propre.*

We are born twice; first to exist, then to live; once as to species, afterwards as to sex. Those who consider women as imperfect men are certainly wrong, though outward resemblance favours the opinion. Till puberty there is no apparent difference: face, form, complexion, even voice, are all nearly alike; girls are children, so are boys; the same name serves for creatures so alike. . . .

But man was not born to remain a child for ever. Nature prescribes a time when childhood ends; and this critical period, short though it be, has far-reaching consequences. As the roaring of the sea foretells the coming storm, so is this tempestuous revolution foretold by a murmuring of the passions. A dull heaving warns

179

us of the approach of danger. A change of disposition, frequent outbreaks of passion, and a constant agitation of mind make the pupil almost impossible to control. He becomes deaf to the voice that used to tame him; like a lion in his fury, he disdains his guide, he refuses to be led. . . .

The second birth has come; now is man truly born to live and "nothing human is strange to him." Hitherto our care has been child's play; now it is serious earnest. The time when ordinary education ends is the time when ours must begin; but, in order to form a clear idea of our new scheme, we must for a moment glance back at the earlier period.

Our passions are the chief instruments of our preservation; it is therefore idle and absurd to try to eradicate them; it is finding fault with Nature, improving the work of God! . . . To hinder the growth of the passions is in my opinion almost as absurd an attempt as to try entirely to destroy them; and those who imagine this to have been my intention have grossly mistaken my meaning. But, because it is man's nature to have passions, would it be reasonable to conclude that all the passions which we feel within ourselves or perceive in others are natural? Their source indeed is natural, but the stream has been swollen by a thousand tributaries; it is a great river constantly growing, in which it would be hard to find one drop of the original spring. Our natural passions are extremely limited; they are the instruments of our liberty and tend to our preservation. The passions which enslave and ruin us spring from another source; Nature does not bestow them, we adopt them to her prejudice.

The source of our passions, the origin and chiefest of all, which alone is born with man and never leaves him,

is love of self (*amour de soi*). This is the original innate
passion, prior to all others; and in a sense all the rest
are only modifications of it. Thus they may all, in a
sense, be considered natural. But most of these modifications proceed from external causes, apart from which
they would never have occurred; far from being advan-
tageous, they are harmful to us; they change and
counteract their first and principal aim; and thus men
become unnatural and act inconsistently with their own
nature.

Love of self is always right, always beneficial. As
every individual is especially charged with his own preservation, his first and greatest anxiety is and ought to
be to watch over it continually; and how could he do
this so well, if it were not his chief interest? Self-
preservation then requires that we love ourselves, nay
that we love ourselves better than anything else, and, as
an immediate consequence, that we love everything which
conduces to our preservation. All children are attached
to their nurses; Romulus must have been attached to
the wolf that suckled him. At first this attachment is
merely physical; whatever contributes to an individual's
welfare attracts him; whatever is prejudicial to it repels
him. This is merely a blind instinct; but instinct is trans-
formed into sentiment, attachment into love, aversion into
hatred, by a manifest intention either to injure us or to
serve us. . . .

A child, therefore, is naturally inclined to benevolence,
because he sees everyone around him ready to give him
assistance; and from this constant observation he learns
to think favourably of his species. In proportion as he
extends his connexions, his needs, and his dependencies,
active and passive, the idea of his relations to others
awakens, and produces sentiments of duty and prefer-

ence. The child then becomes imperious, jealous, deceitful, and vindictive. If you train him to be obedient, not perceiving the use of your commands, he attributes them to caprice, to a wish to torment him, and he becomes mutinous. If you spoil him, as soon as he meets with opposition, he sees in it an act of rebellion, an intention to oppose him, and he beats the chairs and tables for disobeying him. Love of self, which thinks only of self, is contented when our real wants are satisfied; but self-esteem (*amour propre*), which makes comparisons, is not and cannot be content, because, preferring itself to others, it expects that others too should give it the preference, which is impossible. Thus we see how the kindly and affectionate emotions arise from love of self and the hateful and angry passions from self-esteem. Man is rendered good by having few wants and consequently few occasions to compare himself with others; he is rendered bad by having many wants and attaching great importance to opinion. On this principle it is easy to see that all the passions of men or of children may receive either a good or a bad direction. . . .

As soon as a man has need of a companion of the other sex, he is no longer an unsocial being; his heart is no longer single. All his connexions with his species, all the affections of his soul, are born with this sentiment. . . . The preference which we bestow we wish to be returned; love must be reciprocal. To be loved we must become lovable; to be preferred we must become more lovable than another, than every other, at least, in the eyes of the loved one. Hence our first consideration of our fellow-creatures; hence our first comparisons; hence emulation, rivalry, and jealousy.

A heart overflowing with a new sensation is glad to

diffuse itself to its utmost extent; the want of a mistress soon produces the want of a friend; having felt the pleasure of being loved, we wish to be loved by everyone. . . .

Extend these ideas, and we shall see whence self-esteem acquires the form which we assume to be natural, and how love of self, ceasing to be a purely self-regarding sentiment, becomes pride in great souls and vanity in little souls, and is cherished in both at the constant expense of society.

b. The Sympathetic Virtues.

. . . A youth who has been educated in a happy simplicity is inclined to kind and affectionate emotions by the first impulse of Nature. His sympathetic heart feels the sufferings of his fellows; it leaps with joy at the sight of a companion. He feels shame for giving displeasure, regret for having offended. If the natural warmth of his constitution makes him quick, hasty, and passionate, you will a moment later perceive all the goodness of his heart in the effusion of his repentance. . . . Youth is not the age of revenge and hatred, but of compassion, forgiveness, and generosity. . . . " Strange doctrine!" cries the reader, "I never heard it before." Very possible; your philosophers, educated in the corruption of the colleges, are not in a position to have learned it.

Man is made sociable by his weakness; it is our common misery which inclines our heart to humanity. Every attachment is a sign of insufficiency; if we stood in no need of assistance, we should never think of uniting ourselves to others. From our very infirmities springs our uncertain human happiness. A being absolutely happy must be a solitary being. God alone enjoys absolute happiness; but of that happiness who can form an idea? With imperfect beings, he who wants nothing will love nothing, and I cannot conceive that one who loves nothing can be happy.

Hence it follows that our attachment to our fellows is due rather to our sympathy with their pains than with their pleasures. . . . The sight of happiness is more apt to inspire envy than love. . . . But who does not sympathize with the unhappy sufferer? Who would not release him from his misfortunes if it cost no more than a wish? It is easier to imagine ourselves in the position of the wretched than in that of the happy; we feel that misery touches us more nearly than happiness. Compassion is pleasant because, though we put ourselves in the place of the sufferer, we nevertheless rejoice that his pains are not our own. Envy is painful, because the sight of the happy, so far from making us put ourselves in their place, causes us to regret that we are not in such a position in reality. . . .

If you would awaken and keep alive the first impulses of nascent sensibility in a young man's heart, and incline his disposition towards kindness and benevolence, be careful not to sow the seeds of pride, vanity, and envy by a false account of human happiness; do not show him too soon the pomp of courts, the magnificence of palaces, the charms of entertainments; do not let him appear in polite circles, in brilliant assemblies; do not show him the outside of society till he can appreciate its inner worth. To show him the world before he knows men is not to train him, but to corrupt, to deceive him.

. . . A youth of sixteen knows the meaning of suffering, for he has suffered himself; but he hardly knows that others suffer, for seeing without feeling is hardly knowing; and, as I have often said, a child, unable to

imagine others' feelings, knows no evils but his own.
But, when the first development of his faculties kindles
the fire of imagination, he begins to feel in the person of
others, to be moved by their complaints and to suffer in
their sorrow. It is thus that the sad picture of suffering
humanity should excite in his heart the first feelings of
tenderness that he has ever felt.

[Émile has never counterfeited these feelings before
experiencing them.]

To excite and nourish this growing sensibility, to guide
or follow it in its natural bent, what can we do but
present such objects to our young pupil as will most
effectually expand his feelings, extend them to other
beings and separate him from himself; carefully to
banish those which contract and concentrate the human
heart and press the spring of human selfishness; in
other words to inspire him with kindness, humanity,
compassion, benevolence, and all the kindly attractive
passions which are so pleasing to men; and to stifle
envy, greed, hatred, and all the repellent appetites ?

The preceding reflexions may be summarized in two
or three exact, clear, and obvious maxims :

(1) The human heart does not sympathize with those
who are happier than ourselves, but with those who are
more miserable. . . .

(2) We pity in others only those evils from which we
think that we ourselves are not exempt.

. . . Do not therefore accustom your pupil to look
haughtily down upon the sufferings of the unfortunate
and the labour of the poor : he cannot be taught to pity
them, if he looks on them as strangers. Make him see
that the lot of these unhappy creatures may possibly be
his own, that he is by no means exempt from their

misfortunes, and that a thousand unforeseen and unavoidable events may plunge him at any moment into
equal misery. . . . Above all he must not repeat these
words coldly like his catechism; he must see and feel
human calamities. Terrify his imagination with the
perils by which men are constantly surrounded; let him
see these abysses yawning before him; so that, when he
hears you describe them, he may press close to your
bosom for fear of falling in. . . .

(3) Our pity for the misfortunes of others is not
measured by the quantity of evil, but by the realization
of the sensibility of the sufferer.

. . . Physical evil is more limited than is generally
supposed; it is the memory, which gives it duration,
and the imagination, which pictures it in the future,
which make us really deserving of compassion. . . .

The populace compose the bulk of mankind; the rest
are so few that they are hardly worth counting. Man
is the same in every station; therefore the most
numerous station deserves the most regard. . . . Our
philosophers are always telling us that there is an equal
allotment of happiness and misery in every rank—a
maxim as dangerous as it is absurd. If all mankind are
equally happy, what need is there for me to distress
myself for anyone ? [This theme is elaborated.] Learn
therefore to respect your species. Remember that it is
essentially composed of the peoples; and that, if all the
kings and philosophers were removed, they would
scarcely be missed, and things would go on just as well.
In short, teach your pupil to love all men, even those
who despise them. Let him not rank himself in one
class, but in all. Speak to him of man with tenderness,
even with compassion, but never with contempt. Man,
dishonour not mankind ! . . .

There are people who cannot be moved except by cries and tears; the long silent grief of a distressed heart never drew from them a sigh. . . . They may be just, but never humane, generous, or compassionate. But be not in haste to judge the young by this rule. . . . Their apparent insensibility, proceeding merely from ignorance, will change into compassion, as soon as they see that in human life there are countless evils with which they are unacquainted. . . .

But, says the reader, why this scene of affliction? You must have forgotten your first resolution and the constant happiness which you promised your pupil. . . . No. Let us take two young people at the close of the first stage of their education, entering the world by opposite ways. One mounts at once to the summit of Olympus and mixes in the most brilliant society. He is presented at Court and introduced to the great. . . . You are struck with his first rapture. You think him contented; but look into the state of his mind. You think he enjoys these amusements; I think he suffers under them. . . . Observe him surveying a palace, and you see by his impatient curiosity that he is asking himself why the paternal mansion is not equally magnificent. [After many other instances.] We are too apt to judge of happiness by appearances; we imagine it where it least exists; mirth is a very equivocal sign of happiness. . . . The man who is really happy speaks little and rarely laughs; he, as it were, contracts the circle of happiness round his heart.

[He should therefore be taken back into the country.]

Teachers complain that the natural fire of this age makes youth ungovernable: very true, but it is entirely their own fault. This fire of youth, so far from being an obstacle to his education, is the proper instrument for its accomplishment; it gives you a hold over your pupil's affections when he ceases to be less powerful than yourself. His first affections are the reins with which you should guide all his movements. Before, he was at liberty; now he is enslaved. While he was incapable of affection, he was dependent only on himself and his necessities; the moment he loves, he depends on his attachments. Thus are formed the first bonds which unite him to his species; but do not suppose that his new-born susceptibility will be universal, or that he will conceive any meaning in the word "mankind." His susceptibility will at first be confined to his fellows, and his fellows will not be those who are unknown to him, but those with whom he has connexions, those whom custom has rendered dear or needful, those whom he sees to have familiar ways of feeling and thinking, those who are exposed to the pains and sensible to the pleasures which he has experienced. . . .

In becoming capable of attachment, he becomes sensible of it in others and consequently attentive to the signs of this attachment. Thus you see what a new empire you acquire over him, how you have enslaved his heart before he was aware of it. What will be his feelings, when he begins to think about himself, and discovers the services you have done for him, when he can compare himself with other young people of his age and you with other tutors? I say, "when he discovers"; if you once mention it, he will perceive it no more. If you expect obedience in return for your services, he will suspect that you have been playing him a trick; that, while you were pretending to serve him gratuitously, you have been registering a debt against him; that you have bound him by a contract to which he never consented. . . .

2. Training for Society.

a. History.

We must study society by studying men, and men by studying society. Those who treat morals and politics separately will never be acquainted with either. In the first place, a study of man's primitive relations will show us what sentiments and passions are bound to arise therefrom; next, we learn that the progress of those passions reacts on his relations and determines their number. . . . The man of few desires has relations with few persons. Those who consider our physical needs to be the basis of society are confusing them with our unnecessary desires; they mistake the effect for the cause, and have produced from these premises a continuous chain of false reasoning.

In the state of nature, equality is a real and inviolable fact, the difference between man and man never being great enough to make one dependent on another. In the social state, it is a fictitious and impracticable right; the means intended to maintain it serve only to destroy it. The force of the State joins with the strong to oppress the weak, and destroys the equilibrium which Nature has put between them. From this first contradiction between appearance and reality proceed all the others which are found in society. The many will always be sacrificed to the few, and public to private interests. The specious names of justice and subordination will always be made the instruments of violence and the weapons of wrong. It follows that those distinguished orders of men, which pretend to be useful to the others, are in reality useful only to themselves at the others' expense; we may conclude what consideration they deserve by the laws of reason and justice. It remains to see whether the rank which they have assumed is any more favourable to their own happiness, in order that we may know what judgment we should each form of our own lot. To aid us in this enquiry, we must begin by making ourselves acquainted with the human heart.

If it were a question only of showing our pupil Man in disguise, we might save ourselves the trouble; he will see enough of him without our assistance. But, since the disguise is not the man, and since he ought not to be led astray by appearances, let us paint mankind as they really are, not in order that he may hate them, but rather that he may pity them and not desire to resemble them. . . . With this intent, we must now take a different line from that which we have hitherto followed; we must instruct our pupil rather by the experience of others than by his own. . . . His own companions should be chosen with a view to making him think well of them; but we wish him to know the world well enough to think ill of its doings. He should know that man is naturally good, he should perceive it in his own heart, and should judge of his neighbour by himself; but he should observe how society depraves and corrupts him; he should discover the source of its vices in its prejudices; he should be inclined to esteem individuals, but to despise the mass; he should see that all men wear the same mask, but that some of their faces are much more handsome than the masks which cover them.

[A first-hand acquaintance might corrupt him; a purely abstract treatment is beyond his comprehension.]

To avoid these difficulties, and to make him acquainted with the human heart without endangering his own, I would show him mankind at a distance, in other times and places, that he may be a spectator but not become an actor. This is the moment to introduce history; there he will read the heart of man without lessons in philosophy. As a simple spectator, he will look on men without self-interest and without passion, as their judge, not as their accomplice or as their accuser.

To know men, we must see them act. In the world we hear them talk; their words are open, their actions are concealed, History lifts the veil, and we found our judgment on acts. In history, even their conversations help us to estimate them; for, by comparing their words with their deeds, we see at once what they are and what they would appear to be; the more they disguise themselves, the better they are known.

Unfortunately the study of history is not without dangers and difficulties. It is hard to put ourselves in a point of view from which we can judge our fellows fairly. It is one of the great faults of history that it represents more of its characters from their bad than from their good side. It is interesting only by reason of revolutions and catastrophes: as long as nations increase and prosper in the calm of a peaceable government, history remains silent; it begins to speak only when they cease to be content with their own concerns and begin to interfere with those of their neighbours or to allow their neighbours to interfere with theirs; it brings them into prominence only when they are already declining. All our histories begin where they ought to end. . . . Only bad men are celebrated; the good are forgotten or turned into ridicule.

The historical recital of facts is likewise by no means an accurate picture of what really happened. They change their appearance in the historian's mind, they are bent to his interest and tinctured by his prejudices.

Who can put his reader on the scene of action to see
an event as it happened? Everything is disguised by
ignorance or partiality. How easy it is, without altering
a single fact, by emphasizing or passing over circumstances connected with it, to give innumerable appearances to the same facts. . . .

How often has it happened that a few trees more or
less, a hill upon the right or left, or a sudden cloud of
dust, have turned the scale of victory, and the cause has
remained unknown! Does this prevent the historian
from telling you the reason for the victory or defeat
with as much confidence as if he had been in every part
of the battle? Of what consequence are mere facts,
where the reason remains unknown; or what am I to
learn from events of whose causes I am ignorant? Even
criticism, with all its boasting, is nothing but the art of
conjecture, the art of selecting from a number of lies
that which bears most resemblance to the truth. . . .

It will be urged that historical accuracy is of less
importance than truth of manners and characters; that,
provided we have a faithful delineation of the human
heart, it does not matter whether events are truly re-
ported or not. . . . You are quite right if the portraits
are painted from nature; but, if they are mainly products of the historian's imagination, are we not falling
into the very error which we wished to avoid, and giving
an authority to the historian which we refused to the
tutor? If my pupil is to see nothing but imaginary
pictures, I prefer to sketch them with my own hand, as
they will at least be better adapted to him.

The worst historians for a young reader are those who
give us their opinions. Let him be given facts and form
his own opinions: that is the way in which he will learn
to know mankind. If he is constantly guided by an

author's opinion, he sees only with another's eyes; and, when these are taken away from him, he does not see at all.

I reject modern history, not only because it has no character, all men in our day being alike, but because our historians, intent only on displaying their abilities, think of nothing but highly-coloured portraits, which often bear no resemblance to their originals. The ancients as a rule abound less in portraiture, and show less originality in their judgments but more sense. Yet even among the ancients there is great room for choice, and we should at first choose the simpler rather than the most reflective historians. I would put neither Polybius nor Sallust into the hands of a boy : Tacitus is a book for the old, the young cannot understand him. We must learn to read in the actions of men the outlines of the human heart before we try to fathom it to the bottom. We must learn to read facts well before reading maxims. Philosophy, as it is laid down in maxims, belongs only to experience. The young should never generalize : all their instruction should be contained in particulars.

Thucydides is, in my opinion, the best model for historians; he relates the facts without giving his views; but he omits no circumstance which may serve to direct the reader's judgment. He sets events before our eyes in their entirety; and, so far from interposing his own personality, he carefully conceals it. We seem no longer to be readers, but eye-witnesses. Unfortunately his constant subject is war, and a recital of battles is of all things the least instructive. Xenophon's *Retreat of the Ten Thousand* and Cæsar's *Commentaries* have almost equal merit and the same defect. Honest Herodotus, without portraits and without maxims, but flowing, simple - minded, and full of pleasing and interesting particulars, would perhaps be the best historian, if his details did not frequently degenerate into a childishness which is more likely to vitiate than to improve the taste of youth : it needs discernment to read him.   I take no notice of Livy at present ; he is a politician, a rhetorician, and everything that is unsuitable at this age.

History as a rule is defective in recording only distinct and definite facts to which it can assign a name, place and date; but the slow progressive causes of these facts, to which these cannot be assigned, remain for ever unknown.   How often do we find success or failure in a battle stated as the cause of a revolution which had become inevitable before the battle was fought !   War only reveals events already determined by moral causes, which historians rarely notice.   The philosophic spirit of the present day has directed the reflexions of many writers to this point; but I doubt whether truth has gained by their labours.   A madness for system having seized them all, no one sees things as they are, but as they agree with his own particular system.

To these reflexions we may add that history is a representation of actions rather than of men.   The latter are shown only at certain chosen moments, in full parade uniform.   We see a man only in public life, after he has prepared himself to be seen.   History does not follow him into his house, into his study, into his family circle, among his friends : it paints him only when he is playing a part : it exhibits his costume rather than himself.

I would prefer to begin the study of the human heart with individual biographies; for there the hero cannot conceal himself ; the biographer pursues him everywhere ; he gives him not a moment's repose ; he leaves him no corner in which he may avoid the piercing eye of the spectator; he is best known when he believes himself most concealed. "I like biographers," says Montaigne, "because they are more interested in counsels than in events; they show us what passes within rather than without: Plutarch is the writer after my own heart." I admit that the character of a multitude of men or of a nation is very different from that of an individual man, and that we shall be imperfectly acquainted with the human heart if we neglect to study it also in the group; but it is no less true that we must begin by studying the single man in order to know mankind in general, and that, if we know the propensities of each individual, it will not be difficult to foresee their effects when they are combined in the body of the people.

Here again we are compelled to have recourse to the ancients, partly for the reasons already stated, and partly because all familiar and homely details, however true and characteristic, are banned by the modern style. Hence men are disguised in private no less than in public life. . . . Plutarch's excellence lies mainly in those very details into which we dare not enter. He has an inimitable art of depicting great men doing small things, and he is so happy in his touch that often a word, a smile or a gesture is enough to characterize his hero. . . . Cæsar, in passing through a poor village and talking familiarly with his friends, discloses unintentionally the deceiver, who pretended that he only desired to be on an equality with Pompey.

[A number of other instances are given.]

There are few people in a position to imagine the effect which reading, thus directed, can have on young minds. We are deadened by books from our infancy and are accustomed to read without thinking. We are furthermore less affected because we have within ourselves the same passions and prejudices with which history and life abound; we come to regard every transaction as natural; having deviated from Nature ourselves, we judge of others accordingly. But imagine a youth educated according to my principles; imagine my Émile, for whom eighteen years of earnest care have had as their one object to preserve a sound judgment and integrity of heart; imagine him, when the curtain is raised, casting his eye for the first time on the stage of the world, or rather placed behind the scenes, observing the actors dress and undress, and counting the cords and pullies whose gross prestige deceives the eyes of the spectators. His first surprise will soon be succeeded by emotions of shame and contempt for his species; he will be indignant at the sight of mankind, their own dupes, lowering themselves to such child's play; he will weep to see his brethren tear each other in pieces for mere shadows, and become beasts of prey because they could not be content to be men. Given the natural inclinations of our pupil, if the tutor has any judgment in the choice of books and any capacity for directing the youth in his reflexions, his reading will assuredly be a course of practical philosophy, much better and more intelligible than the idle speculations which confound the minds of our young people in the schools.

[He then suggests how Émile will be affected by various historical characters.]

b. Practical Experience.

Emile, reflecting on his superiority to others, will be tempted to suppose the work of your reason to be the product of his own, and to attribute his happiness to his merit. Mankind, he will say, are fools, but I am wise. . . . He is mistaken, and must be undeceived : or rather the mistake must be prevented, lest it be too late after to correct it.

There is no folly of which a sane man may not be cured except vanity; if anything can correct this fault, it must be experience, which may at least check its growth in the early stages. Do not therefore waste your pains in fine arguments, if you wish to convince your pupil that he is a man like others and is subject to the same frailties. Give him experience of the fact, or he will never learn it. Here is another exception to my own rules. I deliberately expose my pupil to every accident which may convince him that he is no wiser than others. Our adventure with the juggler must be repeated in many forms. I let flatterers take every advantage of him; if wastrels lead him into folly and extravagance, I let him risk the danger; if gamblers entice him to the table, I let him become their dupe; I let them flatter, rob and fleece him; and when, after draining his purse, they end by laughing at him, I thank them in his presence for the lesson which they have been good enough to teach him. . . .

[The tutor must not assume a false dignity,] but the pupil ought not to suppose his tutor as ignorant as himself and as easily imposed on. Such an opinion is in place in a child, who, unable to make comparisons, brings mankind down to his own level and gives his confidence only to those who can so reduce themselves. But a youth as old and as sensible as Émile cannot be so hoodwinked, nor would it be good for him if he could. The confidence which he should feel for his tutor is of another kind; it is founded on the authority of reason and on superiority of knowledge. . . .

The greatest skill of a tutor is in so controlling the situations and in so applying his exhortations that he can foresee when his pupil will yield and when he will persist, so that he may everywhere surround him with lessons of experience without exposing him to too great danger. Warn him of his mistakes before he falls into them, but never reproach him afterwards; for that will only rouse and inflame his self-esteem. A lesson which rouses opposition is worthless. I know nothing more fatuous than to say " I told you so."

The age of faults is the age for fables. In censuring folly under a borrowed mask, you instruct without offending; your pupil perceives that the moral is no lie by its obvious application to his own case. A child who has never been deceived by flattery will not understand the fable which I examined in a former page[1]; but the forward youth who has just been duped by a sycophant sees perfectly well that the raven was a fool. Thus from a fact he draws a maxim; and an experience which he would soon have forgotten is impressed on his memory by the fable. There is no moral instruction which may not be acquired by experience—our own or others. In cases where experience is dangerous, it must be learned from history. Where it may be safely risked, it is best that the young man should gain it for himself, and that the experience should be then converted into a general maxim by means of a fable. I do not mean that these maxims should be emphasized or even stated. Nothing is more absurd than the " morals" with which fables generally end; the moral is, or should be, obvious from the fable itself: why deprive the reader of the pleasure of finding it out? The great art of teaching is to make your pupil enjoy his lesson: how can he enjoy it if his mind remains so passive during your recital that he need do nothing in order to understand. . . .

[1] See pp. 115-118.

It is by doing good that we become good : I know of no method more certain. Employ your pupil in every good action within his power; let the interest of the needy always be his own; let him assist not only with his purse but with his care; let him serve them, protect them, and dedicate his person and his time to their service; let him be their steward; he will never all his life be more nobly employed. . . . But are we to make Émile a knight errant, a redresser of wrongs, a paladin? Shall he intrude into public affairs, play the sage, become the defender of the laws before the powerful—before the magistrates—before the King! Ridiculous names do not alter the nature of things. He will do everything which he knows to be good and useful; he will do no more, and he knows that nothing is good and useful for him which is not suitable to his age. He knows that his first duty is towards himself, that the young ought to be diffident, circumspect, respectful to age, cautious of speaking without cause, modest in matters of indifference, but intrepid in doing well and resolute in speaking the truth. . . .

Émile hates noise and quarrels both among men and animals. He will never set dogs to fight, or a dog to chase a cat. . . . If discord reigns among his companions, he tries to reconcile them; if he sees his fellow-creatures in affliction, he enquires into the nature of their distress; if he see two men quarrelling, he asks the cause of their hostility; if he sees a poor man groan under the oppression of a great and powerful neighbour, he seeks means to relieve him of his trouble.

In order to make a proper use of these dispositions, in a manner suited to his age, we must regulate both his acts of kindness and his knowledge, and we must use his zeal to augment them. I cannot repeat it too often; your lessons to the young should consist of actions rather than of words; let them learn nothing from books which they can learn from experience.

[He then discusses the uselessness of teaching Rhetoric.]

What does a schoolboy care how Hannibal prevailed on his troops to cross the Alps? If, instead of these magnificent harangues, you told him how he could persuade his master to give him a holiday, you may be sure he would pay more attention to your rules.

[A long passage follows to show that the altruistic feelings have now been trained.]

c. Teaching of Religion.

It should be remembered that, as our faculties are confined to sensible objects, they present few occasions for the admission of abstract philosophical notions or of purely intellectual ideas. To acquire these, it is necessary either (1) to disengage ourselves from the body to which we are so firmly attached, or (2) to make a slow and gradual progress from object to object, or (3) to pass from the material to the intellectual world by one gigantic leap. Such a leap is impossible for a child; even men need plenty of ladders, made expressly for the purpose. Our first abstract idea is the first of these ladders; but I cannot easily see how to set about constructing them.

The Incomprehensible Being, in whom everything is comprehended, who gives motion to the universe and orders the whole system of living creatures, is neither visible to sight nor palpable to touch; He escapes the investigation of all our senses. The work is revealed, but the Artist is concealed. It is no small matter even to learn His existence; and, when we have proceeded thus far and ask what He is and where, our minds become confused and bewildered, we can only make conjectures.

Locke would have us begin with the study of spirits and proceed later to that of bodies. This is the method of superstition, of prejudice, of error; it is not that of reason, nor even of nature, till it has been thrown out of gear; it is to shut our eyes in order to learn to see. It is requisite to study the nature of bodies for a long time, if we are to acquire a clear notion of spirits, or even to suspect their existence. The contrary order only serves to encourage materialism.

As our senses are the primary instruments of our knowledge, we have an immediate idea only of sensible and corporeal objects. The word "spirit" has no meaning for those who have never thought philosophically. In the minds of children and of the common people, a spirit is nothing more than a body. Do they not imagine spirits which shout and talk and fight and make a noise? It must be admitted that spirits which have arms and tongues greatly resemble bodies. This is the reason why all nations, not even excepting the Jews, have worshipped corporeal deities. . . . Polytheism was the first religion, idolatry the first worship. Men could only recognize a single God after the generalization of their ideas had gradually progressed to a point when they were able to postulate a first cause, to subsume the whole system of being under a single idea, and to give a meaning to the most abstract of all terms, " substance." Every child who believes in a God is therefore necessarily an idolater, or at least an anthropomorphist; and, when once the imagination has pictured God in visible form, it is very rarely that the understanding will ever form a true conception of Him.

[He then urges the difficulty of giving an explanation of the attributes of God.]

If we speak to them of the power of God, they will think Him to be almost as strong as their father. In all cases their measure of possibilities is limited by their knowledge; they think that everything of which they are merely told must be less than that which they have seen for themselves. If we tried to give an idea of a king to a Swiss peasant, who thinks himself the richest of mankind, he will proudly ask us if a king possesses a hundred cows grazing on the mountains.

I foresee how surprised my readers will be that I have let the first period of my pupil's life pass without once speaking to him of religion. At fifteen he does not know whether he has a soul, perhaps it will be too soon for him to learn it at eighteen; for if he learns it too soon, there is a risk of his never knowing it at all.

If I had to paint a picture of the most deplorable stupidity, I should take for my subject a pedant teaching children their catechism: and were I anxious to make an idiot of a child, I should oblige him to explain what he meant when he said it. It may be objected that the greater part of the dogmas of Christianity are mysteries, and that to expect the human mind to understand them is not so much to expect that children should be men as that men should be more. Before we admit mysteries, we must at least comprehend that they are incomprehensible, and children are not capable even of this conception. At an age when everything is mysterious, there are no such things, properly speaking, as mysteries. . . . What can a child believe when he professes Christianity ? He can believe only what he conceives, and he conceives so little of what he is made to say that, if you tell him the direct opposite, he will adopt the latter dogma as readily as the former. The faith of children and of many men is merely an affair of geography. . . .

Beware of divulging the truth to those who cannot understand it; this is the way to substitute error in its place. It were better to have no idea of God than to entertain mean, fantastic, injurious and unworthy ideas; it is a smaller evil to be ignorant of Him than to insult Him. "I had much rather," says the admirable Plutarch, "that people should believe that there is no such person as Plutarch than that they should say he is unjust, envious, jealous, and so tyrannical as to require of others what he has not left them power to perform."

The great evil of those preposterous images of God which we trace on the minds of children is that they remain indelible all their lives; that, when they are men, they have no truer conceptions of God than they had when they were children. I once knew a very worthy and religious woman in Switzerland, who was so firmly convinced of this truth that she would give her son no early instruction in religion, lest he should be content with these imperfect ideas and neglect the acquisition of more perfect ideas when he grew up. This child never heard the name of God uttered but with love and reverence; and, whenever he began to speak of Him, was immediately silenced, as if the subject were too great and sublime for his comprehension. This reserve excited his curiosity, and his self-esteem aspired after the time when he should be made acquainted with the mystery that was so carefully concealed from him.

[Here follows the "Savoyard Curate's Confession."]

So long as we attach no importance to human authority or to the prejudices of the country in which we are born, the unaided light of reason cannot, in the teachings of nature, lead us further than natural religion, and there I stop with my Émile. If he must have another, I have no longer any right to be his guide; he alone must choose it.

We act in conjunction with Nature; while she is forming the physical man, we are striving to form the moral man; but our progress is at different rates. The body is strong and robust while the mind is still weak and feeble; and, let the art of man do what it will, the sensibility is sure to get the start of reason. To restrain the former and to excite the latter has hitherto been our great care; that the man might be as uniform as possible. By developing his natural powers and by cultivating his reason we have restrained and regulated his growing sensibility. Intellectual ideas have moderated the impression of sensible objects. In ascending to the principle of things we have freed him from the subjection of the senses. It was easy to rise from the study of nature to the search for its Author.

As soon as we have attained to this point, what an additional hold have we gained over our pupil! What new ways have we found to speak to his heart! Then only does he find it his true interest to be virtuous; to do good without regard to men, and without compulsion from the laws. . . .

d. Teaching of Sex.

[This topic plays an all-important part in Book IV.; indeed it would be difficult to exaggerate the extent to which the desire to preserve the pupil from Rousseau's own vicious life determines the whole course of the training. The isolation and the complete dependence of the boy on the tutor may be very largely determined

by this consideration; undoubtedly it runs as a sub-
current through Book IV. and mainly determines the
relation of tutor and pupil at this stage. Here particularly Rousseau believes that the state of Society has
vitiated the inclinations of Nature. As his treatment
has more interest from this point of view of considering
its bearing on the rest of Rousseau's scheme of education
than from anything contained in it for its own sake, a
synopsis with a very few passages will be sufficient.
The first passage on the subject comes between the
selections numbered 1 *a* and 1 *b* above : it deals with the
manner of treating the curiosity of young children on
the birth of children.]

Let your answers be serious, short, and definite, with
no appearance of hesitation. It is needless to add that
they should be strictly true. A single admitted falsehood told by the teacher to the pupil would destroy for
ever the fruits of education. Total ignorance might be
the best solution ; but they should learn betimes what
cannot always be concealed. Nothing should be left to
chance ; if you are not absolutely certain that you can
keep him in ignorance till sixteen, tell him before ten. . . .
The delicacy of expression used by polite people before
children, as it presupposes knowledge which children
should not possess, is highly injudicious. [To enquiries,
a mother should dwell on the pains of child-birth.] The
ideas of pain and death cast a veil of sadness over the
imagination and stifle curiosity : his thoughts centre, not
on the cause, but on the results of child-birth. [Stress
is then laid on the danger of letting children hear loose
talk, etc.]

[The topic is resumed after the section on religious
teaching. He argues that the critical age can be much
postponed, and much of the treatment is based on this—
isolation, occupation, etc. The rest of this long section is

occupied with the influence which the tutor can gain over the pupil during adolescence.]

Hitherto I have restrained him by ignorance; now he must restrain himself by his knowledge. This is the time to give in my accounts to him, to explain to him how his time and mine have been employed; what we owe to each other; all his moral relations, all the engagements he has contracted with others or others with him, to what point he has come in the growth of his faculties, what remains to be done, the difficulties he will meet and the means of surmounting them, in what ways I can still help him and in what he must henceforth rely entirely on himself, and finally the critical point which he has now reached, and all the solid reasons which should lead him to keep the closest watch over himself before listening to his growing desires. Remember that, to guide the man, you must follow a method exactly opposite to that which you used to guide the child. Do not hesitate to instruct him in those dangerous mysteries which for so long you carefully concealed from him. Since he must know them ere long, it is proper that his knowledge should come from you alone.

Many readers may imagine that I mean no more than a transient conversation. Not thus is the human heart governed! There are periods in human life that should never be forgotten; such for Émile is that of the instruction of which I speak. One of the mistakes of the present day is to leave its reasonings too unaided, as if men were pure spirits. In modern times men have no longer any hold over one another but force and interest; the ancients did much more by persuasion and the emotions, because they did not neglect the language of signs. All agreements were concluded with the greatest solemnity, in order to render them the more inviolable.

The well of oaths, the well of the Seeing and the Living, the old oak of Mamre, the attesting heaps of stones; such were the rude but august monuments of the sanctity of contracts! In the State, subjects were dazzled by the external pomp of royal authority. The emblems of dignity—throne, sceptre, purple robe, crown, diadem—were sacred. The respect shown to the emblems created a veneration for the wearer; without troops or threats, he spoke and was obeyed.

I shall not rush to Émile's room and make a long dry discourse. I shall begin by stirring his imagination; I shall choose the time, the place and the objects most likely to favour the right impression; I shall invite all nature, as it were, to be witness to our discourse; I shall call on the Eternal Being, whose work it is, to attest its truth; I shall take Him for a judge between us; I shall mark the place where we are, the surrounding rocks, groves, and hills, as monuments of our mutual engagements. In telling him all I have done for him, I shall speak as if I had done it for myself; he will see in my tender affection the reason of my cares. Instead of narrowing his heart by continually talking of his own interest, I intend henceforth only to mention my own. "My child, my joy, my work; it is in your happiness that I look for my own; if you disappoint my hopes, take twenty years off my life; you make my old age miserable!" . .

I have not the least doubt that he will himself come to the point to which I wish to bring him, will eagerly put himself under my protection, and, alarmed at the perils which surround him, will say with all the fire of youth, "My friend, my protector, my master! Resume the authority you wish to resign. . . ." But take care you do not too quickly take him at his word, lest, if ever your yoke appears too heavy, he think himself entitled to shake it off, on the ground that he has been taken by surprise. . . .

As soon as my authority is established, my first care will be to guard against any need of using it. I shall spare no pains to establish myself in his confidence, to become more and more the confidant of his feelings, and to be the arbiter of his pleasure. Instead of opposing, I shall consult his youthful inclinations, in order to have them under my direction; I shall enter into his designs to the 'end that I may conduct them; and I shall not endeavour to procure him a distant good at the expense of his present happiness.

3. Émile's Entrance into Society.

a. His actual Conduct in Society.

Émile was not formed to live in solitude; as a member of society, he must fulfil its functions. Framed to live with men, he must know them. He knows mankind in general; he must now learn to know them as individuals. He knows what men do in the world; he must now learn how they live. It is time to show him the outside of this great stage, of which he already knows the hidden machinery. . . . Whoever learns to know the world too young, will follow its usages without reflexion or choice all his life; and, despite his conceit, without knowing the real nature of his acts. But the man who learns these lessons at a time when he can see the underlying reasons will follow them with more discernment, and consequently more accurately and with a better grace. . . . Introduce a youth into the world at twenty, and under good direction he will become more amiable and more judiciously polished in a year than his neighbour who has been bred there from infancy. The former can see the reasons for our behaviour in relation to age, to station and to sex, can reduce them to principles, and can extend them to unforeseen cases; whereas the latter, having only routine to guide him, is puzzled as soon as he leaves the beaten track. In France, young ladies are educated in convents till they marry; have they any difficulty in learning the manners of society?

[Neither must it be postponed too late. On his entrance into society, the tutor thus addresses the pupil:—]

"Your heart needs a companion; let us go in search of one suitable. Perhaps it will not be easy to find her; real merit is always scarce; let us not be in a hurry, neither let us be discouraged. No doubt she exists, and we shall find her at last, or at least the most like her. . . ." I should be the most awkward of men, if I did not make him fall in love with her without knowing who she was. It does not matter whether the object of my description is imaginary; it is enough if it makes him dislike every other who might tempt him, if, wherever he goes, he prefers his chimera to the real objects that will meet his eyes. . . . I would go so far as to name her; I should say with a smile, "Let us call your love Sophie; Sophie is a name of good augury; if your choice does not bear that name, at least she will be worthy of it. . . ." After these particulars, if, without affirming or denying, you escape by evasions, his suspicions will be changed into certainty; he will really believe that you are making a mystery of the lady whom you design to be his wife, and that he will see her in due time. When once you have led him thus far, if you have wisely chosen the points to emphasize, the rest is easy; you may introduce him into the world almost without danger.

[Most of the debauchery of French youths is a fashion; Émile has been trained to rely on his own judgment.]

Into whatever rank he was born, into whatever society he is introduced, his entrance will be plain and simple: and please God he be not so unhappy as to shine! He neither has nor wishes to have the qualities which strike at first sight. . . . His manner of saluting is neither shy nor vain, but natural and true; he knows no restraint or disguise; in the midst of an assembly, he is just the same as when he is alone. . . . He neither disputes and contradicts, nor cringes and flatters: he states his own opinion without attacking those of others; for he loves liberty above everything, and freedom of speech is one of its chief prerogatives. He says little, because he does not care that others should think about him; for the same reason he says nothing but what is useful, for what other motive could make him speak? . . . Far from shocking the prejudices of others, he conforms to their habits willingly enough; not with a view of appearing well acquainted with them or of affecting the airs of a man of the world, but on the contrary to avoid notice: he is never more content than when people pay no attention to him. Though at his entrance into the world he is totally unacquainted with its manners, he is not for that reason shy or nervous. If he conceals himself, it is not owing to embarrassment, but because, to see well, a person must not be seen. What others think of him does not give him the least uneasiness; nor is he at all afraid of ridicule. . . . Towards the other sex, I believe he will be sometimes timid and bashful; but surely this bashfulness will not be disagreeable to them. . . . No-one will be more exact in all the rules of decorum which are founded on nature or even on the well-being of society; but he will prefer the former to the latter; thus

he will pay a far greater respect to a private person who
is older than himself than to an official of his own
age. . . . He will be, if you will, an amiable stranger.
At first they will excuse his singularities and say " He
will improve." When they become accustomed to his
conduct and see that he does not change, they will continue to excuse him by saying " He was made so."

b. Study of Literature.

While studying men by their behaviour in the world,
as he formerly studied them by their passions in history,
he will have frequent occasion to reflect on the objects
which gratify or displease our feelings. He will in fact
be considering the philosophy of taste, a study suited to
his present period of life.

The further we go in search of a definition of taste, the
more we are bewildered; taste is only the power of judging what will please or displease the greatest number.
Go beyond that and no definition is possible. It does
not follow that men of taste constitute the majority; for,
although a majority form a correct judgment on each
subject, there are few who agree with the majority on
every subject; and, though the most general agreement
of tastes constitutes good taste, yet there are few people
of taste; just as there are but few handsome persons,
though beauty is only a union of the most ordinary
elements. . . .

Taste is natural to all mankind, but they do not all
possess it in the same degree. . . . The degree of taste
which is possible for us depends on our innate sensibility;
its development and form depend on the societies in
which we live. First, we must live in large societies, to
make many comparisons : secondly, they must be societies
of amusement and idleness, for those of business are not

regulated by pleasure, but by self-interest: thirdly, they must be societies in which there is not too great an inequality, where the tyranny of opinion is moderate, and where pleasure is more predominant than vanity; for, where it is otherwise, fashion destroys taste, and we no longer look for objects which please us, but for those which win us distinction. . . .

The works of men are beautiful only by imitation. All true models of taste are to be found in Nature. The further we deviate from the master, the more do our copies degenerate. We take our models from the objects which we love; or, if beauty of imagination is subjected to caprice and authority, from the objects which are approved by our guides. Our guides are the artists, the great and the wealthy; and their guides are self-interest and vanity. The wealthy wish to display their wealth, and the artists to win a share of it: thus they compete with one another in the search after new methods of expense. Henceforth luxury establishes its sway; we come to admire the costly and difficult; beauty is found in contradicting, not in imitating, Nature. Luxury and bad taste are inseparable; wherever taste is expensive, it is false. . . .

Consult the taste of women in physical matters, which pertain to the judgment of the senses, and that of men in moral matters, which are more dependent on the understanding. . . .

If, in training my pupil's taste, I had to choose between those countries where taste had yet to be formed and those where it had already degenerated, I should proceed backwards, beginning with the latter and ending with the former. My reason is that vitiation of taste proceeds from an excessive delicacy in distinguishing shades of difference which escape a more obtuse gaze, and that this delicacy leads to a spirit of criticism. Discrimination reveals variety; it increases shades of feeling and renders taste less uniform, till at last there are as many tastes as there are critics. Through the disputes on the merits of these tastes, knowledge and criticism are extended, and we learn to think. Delicate observation is only possible among persons of wide experience, because it is a late development; and persons unaccustomed to large societies confine their attention to broader features. Perhaps there is no civilized town where the general taste is worse than in Paris; yet this is the capital where good taste is trained, and few books of note have lately been written in Europe of which the author has not been to Paris to form his taste. Those who think it enough to read Parisian books are mistaken; far more is learned from the conversation of authors than from their books; and authors are not the persons from whom you learn most. It is the spirit of societies which developes our intellectual powers and extends our vision as far as it will reach. If you have a spark of genius, spend a year in Paris: you will soon be all that you are capable of becoming—or else you will never be anything at all.

You may learn to think in places where bad taste prevails; but you must not think like those who are infected with it, though it is difficult to avoid this danger if you reside among them too long. . . . I shall take care not to refine Émile's judgment so far as to transform it: and when his discrimination has become delicate enough to distinguish and to compare the different tastes of mankind, it will be on more simple objects that I shall lead him to base his own. . . .

This is the time for reading and for agreeable books, for teaching him to analyze a discourse, and for initiating him into all the beauties of eloquence and style. It is little use learning languages for their own sake; their value is not so important as people imagine; but the study of languages leads to that of general grammar. You must learn Latin properly to know French; you must study and compare both languages to understand the rules of speech.

Besides, there is a certain compelling simplicity of taste which is found only in the writings of the ancients. In oratory, in poetry, in every kind of literature, as well as in history, he will find them abounding in matter but sparing of reflexions. Modern authors on the contrary say little and generalize much. To be perpetually giving us their judgment as law is not the way to form our own. The difference of taste in the two periods is evident in public monuments and even on tomb-stones. Ours are covered with eulogiums; on theirs you might read facts. . . . "Traveller, go tell Sparta we died here to obey her holy laws": you can see that these words were not written by the Academy of Inscriptions.

As my pupil sets so little value on words, I am much mistaken if his attention is not directed to these differences and if they do not influence his choice of authors. Struck with the masculine eloquence of Demosthenes, he will say, "This is an orator": reading Cicero, he will remark, "This is a pleader."

Émile will generally prefer the writings of the ancients, if only for this reason, that, coming earlier, they were nearer Nature and had more invention. Let la Motte and the Abbé Terrasson say what they will, there is no real advance in reason among men; what is gained in one way is lost in another. We all start from the same point; and, as the time which we spend on the thoughts of others is not available to learn how to think for ourselves, we possess more second-hand knowledge and less originality. . . .

Having thus made my pupil mount to the springs of pure literature, I likewise show him the stagnant waters in the reservoirs of modern compilers—journals, translations, and dictionaries; upon all these he will cast an eye, and then leave them for ever. . . .

I take him to the theatre to study, not manners, but taste: to those who are capable of reflexion taste is best shown in the theatre. "Lay precepts and morals aside," I should say to him, "they are not to be learned here. The stage was not made to exhibit truth, but to please and amuse; there is no other place where you can so easily learn the art of pleasing and interesting the human heart. The study of the stage leads to that of poetry; for both have the same object. If he has but the least spark of taste for it, with what pleasure will he cultivate the poetical languages, Greek, Latin and Italian! These studies will be recreation, not forced work, and will be for this reason the more valuable; they will be his delight at an age and amid circumstances when the heart is so keen in the pursuit of every kind of beauty which is able to attract it. Contrast Émile and a school-boy when they read Tibullus or Plato's *Symposium*, or the fourth book of the *Æneid!*

My chief design in teaching him to feel and to love the beautiful in all its manifestations is to fix thereon his affection and taste to prevent a change of his natural inclinations and to hinder him from ever seeking in wealth a happiness which he can find within himself. I have observed elsewhere that taste is no more than self-knowledge in regard to little things. This is very true; but, since it is on the sum of little things that the pleasure of life depends, attention to them is by no means a trivial matter. From it we learn to drink deep of the good things which lie within our reach and to drain from them all the meaning which they can have for us. I am not speaking of moral good, which depends on the disposition of the mind, but only of the domain of the senses—of real pleasure as opposed to prejudice and opinion.

[The book concludes with a long section containing a plea for simplicity of life, the author showing how little pleasure is gained from various conventional luxuries.]

VIII

EDUCATION OF GIRLS

1. Systematic Account: Émile, Book V., Part I.

a. Characteristics and Duties of Women.

Sophie must be a woman as Émile is a man; that is, she must be endowed with every quality suited to her species and to her sex, in order to take her place in the physical and moral order. Let us begin by examining the resemblances and differences between her sex and our own.

In everything that does not pertain to sex, woman is man; in everything that pertains to sex, man and woman have at every point resemblances and differences. Comparison is difficult, because it is hard to determine what characteristics do or do not pertain to sex. Many broad differences, which do not at first appear related thereto, are in reality connected with it by ties which we are unable to discover. These relations and differences must influence character. This consequence is obvious and conforms to experience. Hence we see the idleness of the dispute concerning the superiority or equality of the sexes; as if each by pursuing the intent of nature according to its own destination were not more perfect on that account than if it bore a greater resemblance to

the other. In their common qualities, they are equal;
in regard to their differences, they do not admit of a
comparison; a perfect woman and a perfect man ought
not to resemble one another in mind any more than in
face, and perfection does not admit of degrees of comparison. . . .

Woman was made specially to please man; if the
latter must please her in turn, it is a less direct necessity;
his merit consists in his strength, he pleases by that fact
alone. This is not the law of love, I grant; but it is the
law of nature, which is antecedent even to love. If
woman is formed to please and to live in subjection, she
must render herself agreeable to man instead of provok-
ing his wrath; her strength lies in her charms.

There is no sort of parity between man and woman as
to the importance of sex. The female is female all her
life, or at least all her youth. Everything incessantly
reminds her of her sex; and, to discharge her duties
well, her whole mode of life must be relative to them.
She needs care during her pregnancy, and an easy
sedentary life while nursing her children; to bring them
up, she requires patience and sweetness, zeal, and an
affection which nothing can discourage: she is the bond
which connects the children with their father; she
alone can make him love them and inspire him with
confidence to call them his own. What tenderness
and care must she not exert to preserve unity in the
family! . . .

Is a woman able to pass by sudden alterations from
one mode of life to another without risk or danger?
Can she be a nurse to-day, an Amazon to-morrow? Can
she change her tastes and inclination as a chameleon
changes its hue? Shall she pass suddenly from the
domestic hearth and the guidance of her family to be

buffeted by the weather, to endure work, fatigue and the dangers of war? Shall she be now timorous, now intrepid, at one time delicate, at another robust?

b. Educational Corollaries.

When once it is shown that men and women neither are nor ought to be constituted alike either in character or in temperament, it follows that they ought not to receive the same education. In pursuance of the dictates of nature, they ought to act in concert, but not to be employed in the same operations; their work may be directed to the same end, but should be different in itself, and so should be the tastes which direct it. We have tried to form the natural man; for fear lest our work remain imperfect, let us see how to train a woman that shall match him.

If you wish to be always under proper guidance, always follow the indications of nature. The distinguishing marks of the sex ought to be respected as nature's ornament. I hear you continually saying, "Women have this or that defect from which we are exempt." Your pride deceives you; they would be defects in you, but they are characteristics of women; the world would not be so well constituted if women did not possess these qualities. Prevent these pretended defects from degenerating, but take care not to destroy them.

Women on the other hand are apt to complain that we bring them up to be vain and coquettish, and that we continually amuse them with frivolities in order the more easily to remain their masters; in short, they throw back on us the blame for the imperfections of which we accuse them. What folly! How long is it since men have concerned themselves with the education of girls? Who debars their mothers from bringing them up in whatever manner they please? . . . The more their sex tries to resemble ours, the less influence they will have over us; and then it is that we shall be really their masters.

The several abilities common to the two sexes are not equally distributed, but in the final result the differences are compensated; woman counts for more as woman and less as man; wherever she asserts her own rights, she has the advantage of us; wherever she attempts to usurp ours, the advantage is on our side. This general truth can only be contradicted by alleging exceptions, a manner of arguing constantly used by gallant admirers of the fair sex.

To cultivate in woman the qualities of man and to neglect her own is therefore evidently to act to her prejudice. . . . But does it follow that a woman ought to be brought up in absolute ignorance and confined entirely to the management of a household? Shall man make a servant of his help-mate and deprive himself in her company of the greatest charm of society? The better to keep her in subjection, shall he debar her from all feeling and knowledge? Will he make her a mere machine? No, surely; this was never the intention of Nature in endowing her with so delightful and imaginative a mind; on the contrary, Nature intends that she should think, should judge, should love, should learn, and should improve her understanding as she improves her person: these are the arms with which she has supplied her, to compensate for the strength which she lacks, and to control that which we possess. She ought to learn many things, but only such as are of use to her to know. . . .

On the good constitution of mothers depends in the

first instance that of their children; on the care of women depends the first education of men; on women also depend our manners, our passions, our tastes, our pleasures, and even our happiness. Thus the whole education of women should be relative to men. To please them, to be useful to them, to win their love and esteem, to bring them up when young, to tend them when grown, to advise and console them, and to make life sweet and pleasant to them; these are the duties of women at all times, and what they ought to learn from infancy. Unless we are guided by this principle, we shall miss our aim, and all the instructions which we bestow on them will contribute neither to their happiness nor to our own. . . .

c. Early Studies: Needlework.

Little girls, almost from their cradle, love dress; not content with being pretty, they wish to be thought so. . . . From whatever quarter girls receive this first lesson, it is a very good one. Since the body is, in a sense, born sooner than the mind, it needs to be trained earlier. This priority of bodily training is common to both sexes, but it is directed to a different object. In the case of boys the object is to develop strength, in the case of girls to bring out their charms. Not that these characteristics ought to be exclusively confined to one sex, but that there is an inversion of their importance. Women need enough strength to act gracefully, men enough skill to act easily.

An exaggerated delicacy in women spreads to men. Women should not be vigorous to the same extent as men; but they need vigour for the sake of men, that is to say, in order to secure vigour in their offspring. In this respect the convents, where the boarders receive a simple diet but obtain plenty of recreation, of open-air games and of running in the garden, are preferable to most homes, where the daughters are daintily fed, are always being coaxed or scolded, and have not a moment's liberty to play, to jump or to run about, to make a noise, or to indulge in any of those little levities which are so natural to their age. [He then praises the Spartan education.]

Children of both sexes have, and ought to have, many amusements in common; is it not the same when they are grown up? But there are also special tastes which distinguish each sex. Boys like movement and noise— drums, tops and hobby-horses; girls prefer decorations that please the eye—looking-glasses, jewellery, baby-clothes, and particularly dolls. Dolls are the favourite amusement of little girls—a taste clearly based on their life-work. The physical part of the art of pleasing consists in dress, and this is the only part that children can learn. A girl will spend the whole day with her doll. . . . But you will say, "She dresses her doll, not herself." No doubt; she sees her doll and does not see herself. . . . Here we have therefore an innate and distinctly marked taste : you have only to follow it and to direct it. It is certain that the little girl will wish with all her heart to know how to decorate her own doll, to make its top-knots, its handkerchief, its furbelow, its lace; she is made so entirely dependent on the good-will of others that she would love to be indebted to nothing but her own industry. This suggests the guiding principle of her first lessons; they will be given, not as prescribed tasks, but as special favours. Indeed most little girls dislike learning to read and write, but exhibit the greatest pleasure in learning the use of a needle. They imagine themselves already grown women; they are delighted with the notion that these abilities can one day be employed on their own persons. . . . Both sexes indeed ought to confine their studies to practical knowledge, but it is a more necessary rule in the case of women; a woman's work, though less laborious, is or ought to be more continuous and more varied; she cannot indulge a hobby to the prejudice of her domestic duties.

Girls are generally more docile than boys, and, as I shall shortly explain, we ought to make more use of authority with them: but it does not follow that we should make any requirement from them of which they do not see the utility. The art of mothers consists in pointing out the utility of all which they prescribe; and this is the easier, as the understanding ripens much earlier in girls than in boys. . . . If I am unwilling that compulsion should be used to make a boy learn to read, I have much stronger reasons against compelling a girl, until she clearly realizes its use. . . . Perhaps she should learn arithmetic before anything else; for nothing is more obviously of general use, nothing needs longer practice, and nothing gives more opportunities for mistakes than accounts.

d. Moral Discipline; Constraint.

Always justify the tasks which you impose on young girls, but never fail to impose them. Idleness and want of docility are their two most dangerous faults, and the hardest to cure if once they have been allowed to grow. Girls ought to be energetic and industrious, but this is not all; they should at an early age be inured to constraint. This evil, if in their case it is an evil, is inseparable from their condition. They will all their lives be subjected to an unceasing and unyielding constraint, that of convention. They must therefore be accustomed to restriction from the first, that it may cost them nothing; their fancies must be crushed, to subject them to the will of others. If they wish always to be at work, they ought sometimes to be compelled to do nothing. . . .

A girl who loves her mother or her aunt will work with her all day without being tired; the chat alone makes amends for the restraint. . . . Girls who do not prefer the company of their mothers to any other society will never turn out well; but, if we wish to judge of their real feelings, we must watch them, and not merely rely on what they say; for they are full of deceit and flattery, and learn very early to dissimulate. Nor should we bid them love their mothers as a duty; affection does not spring from duty; it is a matter in which compulsion has no place. Attachment, tenderness and habit are enough to make a girl love her mother, unless the latter has done something to incur her aversion. Even the very restraint in which she is kept will, if properly directed, strengthen rather than weaken this inclination; for dependence is women's natural lot, and girls feel that they were made in order to obey.

As they have or should have very little liberty, they are inclined to carry that little to excess; extreme in everything, they give themselves up even more wholeheartedly to their amusements than do boys. . . . This eagerness ought to be checked; for it is the cause of many faults peculiar to women, among others of that capricious fascination which infatuates them to-day with something which they will not notice to-morrow. Fickleness in their tastes is as fatal as excess; and both are derived from the same source. Do not debar them from gaiety and laughter, from noise and merry games; but see that they do not become so surfeited with one amusement that they hurry away to another; do not suffer them to be free from restraint a single moment of their lives. Accustom them to be called away in the middle of their play and to return to their work without a murmur. Habit will suffice for the purpose, because in this case it merely reinforces Nature.

From this habitual constraint arises a docility which women need all their lives, since they never cease to be subject either to a man or to the opinions of men, and they are never suffered to render themselves independent of those opinions. The first and most important attribute to a woman is good temper: formed to obey so imperfect a being as man, a being often so full of vices and always of imperfections, she ought to learn betimes to submit even to injustice, and to bear oppression from her husband without complaining.

[He then discusses ingenuity in pleasing and extravagance in dress.]

e. Teaching of "Accomplishments."

The first thing which girls discover as they grow older is that all their external ornaments are insufficient unless they have some that are personal. Beauty cannot be acquired; coquettry requires time to develope; but they may strive to give grace to their gestures, to speak in a pleasing tone, to acquire a composed bearing, to walk lightly, to throw themselves into graceful attitudes and to choose every advantage to set off their person. . . .

I am aware that strict tutors are opposed to teaching young girls singing, dancing, or any of the agreeable accomplishments. This is absurd. Who then is to learn them? Boys? For whom are these arts more important, for men or for women? You may say, "For neither.

To sing profane songs is a crime; dancing is an invention of the devil; a girl ought to have no occupation but work and prayer." Strange employments for a child of ten! For my part, I am much afraid that those little saints who are compelled to spend their childhood in prayer will occupy their youth in a very different manner, and will do their best, when they are married, to make up for the time which they feel that they have lost when they were girls. We should regard age as well as sex; a young girl ought not to live like her grandmother, she should be lively and cheerful, play, dance and sing as much as she pleases, and taste all the innocent pleasures of her age: the time will come too soon to be sedate and to put on a more serious demeanour. . . .

The agreeable accomplishments are treated too much as if they were serious pursuits; they have been over-systematized: everything has been reduced to maxim and precept, and young people are painfully bored by what was intended only for their amusement and diversion. Nothing can be imagined more ridiculous than an old music or dancing master frowning on young people who wish only to laugh, and assuming a more pedantic and magisterial air in teaching his trifling art than if he were instructing them in their catechism. Does singing, for instance, need written music? Is it not possible to render the voice flexible and accurate, to learn to sing with taste, and even to accompany, without knowing a single note? . . .

It is often asked whether girls should be taught by masters or mistresses. I do not know; I should be glad if they needed neither. It would be better if they learned informally what they have so strong an inclination to learn, and if fewer laced dancing masters were seen strolling about our towns. . . . In arts which have no object but pleasure, anyone may serve as teacher, their father, mother, brother, sister, friends or tutors, their looking-glass, or preferably their own taste. Do not offer to teach them, but wait for them to ask : we ought not to turn a reward into a task; and this is precisely the kind of study in which the wish to succeed is the beginning of success. If we must have formal lessons, I will not determine which sex is to give them. . . .

Speech occupies the first place among the pleasing accomplishments; by this means alone can we enhance those charms to which the senses are already accustomed. . . . This, I imagine, is the reason why girls so soon acquire a pretty manner of prattling, that they employ the right expression even before they know its meaning, and that we enjoy listening to them so long before they can understand our conversation. . . . Man says what he knows, woman what she pleases; in order to speak, a man needs knowledge, a woman needs taste; the chief aim of man ought to be the useful, of women the agreeable. Their discourse should have nothing in common save truth. We ought not therefore to restrain the prattle of girls like that of boys with the harsh question, "Of what use is that?" but by another question, which indeed is no easier to answer, "What effect will that produce?" At this early period, while they are still unable to discern good and bad, and cannot estimate anyone's conduct, they should make it an invariable rule never to say anything disagreeable; but this rule is harder to practise, because it is always subordinate to another, which is never to tell an untruth.

f. Teaching of Religion.

If boys are incapable of forming a true idea of religion, we can imagine that this idea is still more unsuited to the comprehension of girls; yet for this very reason I should speak to them much sooner on the subject. . . . Since a woman's conduct is subject to public opinion, her belief is subject to authority. Every girl ought to follow the religion of her mother and every married woman that of her husband. Even if this religion be false, the submission with which the wife and daughter obey the order of nature cancels, in the sight of God, the sin of ignorance. . . .

Since the religion of women is to be regulated by authority, our aim is not so much to explain to them the reasons for their belief as to give them a concise account of the belief itself; for a belief in obscure ideas is the first source of fanaticism: and to demand a belief in absurdities leads either to folly or to incredulity. I do not know whether our catechisms have a greater tendency to irreligion or to fanaticism; but I am very well satisfied that they are necessarily productive of one or of the other.

In the first place, in teaching religion to young girls, do not make it an object of gloom or boredom, a task or a duty; do not therefore make them learn anything connected with it by heart, not even their prayers. . . . It is not so important that young girls should know their religion early as that they should know it well, and above all that they should love it. . . . When you explain to them the articles of faith, do it by means of direct instruction and not by questions and answers.

[A long model of a conversation is given leading up to the idea of a Creator.]

It remains to observe that, till the age when reason awakes and nascent sensibility unseals the lips of conscience, young persons have no notion of good and

evil but that which is derived from the statements of
those about them. What they are commanded is good;
what they are forbidden is bad; that is all they ought
to know. This shows that it is even more important in
the case of girls than of boys, to choose the right persons
who should approach them and have authority over
them.

g. Special Characteristics of Women's Intellect.

I have already perhaps said too much upon this
subject. To what shall we reduce women if we allow
them no other law than general prejudice? Let us not
so far debase the sex which governs us, and which
honours us—if we do not degrade it. The whole human
species has a guide anterior to opinion. To the invariable direction of this guide all others ought to be
reduced; it pronounces judgment even on prejudice
itself; and the authority of human opinion ought to
extend only so far as it agrees with it.

This guide is the inner sensibility. I shall not repeat
what has been said above; it is enough for me to
observe that, unless these two sanctions concur, the
education of women will certainly be defective. Sensibility, apart from opinion, will not give them that
delicacy of mind which wins for virtue the honour of the
world; and opinion without sensibility will only render
women false and dishonest and will substitute appearance
in the place of virtue.

They are therefore obliged to cultivate a faculty which
shall serve as an umpire between these two guides, which
shall rectify the errors of prejudice and shall prevent the
conscience from being misled. This faculty is reason.
But at the bare mention of the word, what questions
arise! Are women capable of solid reasoning? Is it

important for them to cultivate it? Will its cultivation bear fruit? Is it of use in the duties assigned to them? Is it consistent with the simplicity which becomes them?

The different ways of treating and answering these questions have driven many persons to opposite extremes. Some are for confining a woman to the needle and distaff in company with her maids, and thus make her only the first servant to her lord; others, not content with safeguarding her own rights, allow her likewise to usurp ours; for to leave her our superior in the qualities which are peculiar to her sex and to render her our equal in all the rest is to transfer to the wife the supremacy which Nature has given to the husband.

The type of Reason which leads men to a knowledge of their duties is not very complex; that which leads a woman to understand hers is still simpler. The obedience and fidelity which she owes her husband, the care and tenderness which she owes her children are such natural and obvious consequences of her position that she cannot sincerely refuse her consent to the sensibility which guides her, nor can she mistake her duty unless her inclinations are already corrupted. . . .

As she is subject to men's judgment, she should deserve their esteem; she ought especially to obtain that of her husband; not only should she make him love her person, but likewise approve her conduct; she ought to justify his choice in the eyes of the public, and win for her husband the respect which is paid to his wife. How can she accomplish this if she is ignorant of the means— if she knows nothing of our customs and proprieties—if she does not recognize the source of human opinions nor the passions by which they are determined? As she is dependent both on her own conscience and on the

opinions of others, she must learn to compare and to
reconcile these two guides, and to prefer the former
when they are opposed. She passes judgment on her
own judges; she determines when she ought to obey
them and when she ought to refuse. Before she admits
or rejects their prejudices, she learns to trace them to
their source, to anticipate them, and to make them
favourable to her; she is careful never to incur censure,
when her duty permits her to avoid it. Nothing of this
kind can be done without cultivating her reason and
understanding. . . .

[He then describes the peculiar genius of women,
illustrating the tact of a hostess at dinner to her guests,
and proceeding:—]

When they are all gone, the husband and wife talk of
what has happened. The man repeats the gossip of the
table and what has been said or done by those with
whom he has conversed. If the wife is not always the
most exact on these points, on the other hand she has
noticed what was whispered quite softly at the other end
of the room; she knows what So-and-so was thinking;
to what such and such a discourse or gesture related; in
short, there has scarcely been a significant movement
which she is not ready to explain, and nearly always to
explain rightly. . . .

Is this sagacity acquired ? No, it is innate in women;
they all possess it; and men never have it in the same
degree. This is one of the distinctive characteristics of
the sex. Presence of mind, sagacity, and delicate
observation are woman's special branch of knowledge;
skill in using them is their particular art. . . .

h. Social Training of Women.

From these considerations we may determine in general the kind of education which is suited to women's character, and to what subjects we ought to direct their attention from their childhood. As I said, the duties of their sex are more easily seen than fulfilled. The first thing which they ought to learn is to love these duties from a consideration of their utility; this is the only way to make them easy. Every station and every age has its duties, which it soon learns, provided it loves them. Women, honour your state and, in whatever station Providence places you, you will always be respected. The essential point is to be what Nature made you; you are always only too much what man expects you to be.

Investigation into abstract and speculative truths, into principles and scientific axioms, and everything that tends to generalize our ideas, is not the province of women. Their studies ought to be entirely practical; it is for them to apply the principles which man has discovered and to make observations which help man to establish them. All the reflexions of women on subjects not immediately connected with their duties ought to be directed to the study of man or to the recreative arts which have taste as their object. Works of genius are above their comprehension; they have not enough accuracy and attention to succeed in the exact sciences; and, as for the study of the physical world, it belongs to the sex which is most active, which sees most objects, possesses most strength, and most often exercises it to judge of the laws of nature and of the relations of sensible objects. Woman, being weak and knowing no resources outside herself, estimates and determines means by which she can supplement her weakness; and, these are the passions of men. She has a mechanics more powerful than ours; her levers are employed to move the human heart. Is anything necessary or agreeable to her which her sex cannot procure for itself? She must have the skill to make us desire its accomplishment. For that end she must sound the mind of man to its depths, not the abstract mind of man in general, but the minds of those men by whom she is surrounded, and to whom she is subjected whether by law or by custom. She must learn to discover their sentiments by their conversation, by their actions, by their looks and by their gestures. She must by her own conversation, actions, looks, and gestures know how to inspire them with whatever sentiments she pleases, without appearing to have any such design. Men will philosophize better concerning the human heart; she will be much better able to read it. Women's province is what I may call Experimental Morality; ours is to reduce it to a system. Women have more sagacity, men more genius; women observe, men reason; the combination produces the clearest and most complete idea that the human mind can form of itself; in short it produces the surest knowledge of ourselves and of others that we are capable of acquiring. Thus it is that art is incessantly tending to improve the instrument which Nature has given.

The world is women's book; when they read it amiss, it is their own fault, or they are blinded by some passion. Yet the true mother of a family, far from being a woman of the world, is only less of a recluse in her home than a nun in her cloister. It would be well therefore to act in the same manner towards young women who are going to be married as we act or should act towards those who are about to take the veil; they should be shown the pleasures which they are leaving before they are allowed to renounce them, lest a false representation of these unknown pleasures should some time seduce their hearts and disturb the tranquillity of their retreat. In France girls live in convents and married women in the world. Among the ancients it was quite the contrary: the girls had plenty of games and public festivals; married women lived in retirement. . . .

Mothers! at least make companions of your daughters. Give them right feelings and an honest heart, and then conceal nothing from them that is proper for a chaste eye to behold. Balls, banquets, games, even the theatre, everything that, seen through a wrong medium, deludes imprudent youth, may without risk be exposed to a healthy vision. The earlier they see these tumultuous pleasures, the sooner will they be surfeited with them. . . .

Convents are real schools of coquettry. . . . To love a quiet domestic life, it is necessary to know it and to have felt its pleasures from infancy. Love of home is only learned at home; no woman who was not brought up by her own mother will care to bring up her own children. . . .

It is not necessary to tire young girls with long discourses or to declaim dry moral lectures to them. Moral preachings are, in the case of both sexes, the death of true education. Melancholy instructions only make young people detest those who give them and all which they say. In speaking to girls, there is no occasion to frighten them with their duties, nor to aggravate the yoke which Nature has impressed on them. In explaining their duties, be clear and precise; do not let them believe that their performance is a

gloomy task; do not assume a dismal face nor an air of
severity.   Whatever is to enter the heart of others must
come from your own; their moral catechism should be
as short and as clear as their religious catechism, but it
should not be so grave.   Let them see in those very
duties the source of their pleasures and the foundation of
their rights.   Is it so painful to love in order to be loved,
to be amiable with a view of being happy, to be worthy
of esteem for the sake of being obeyed, to act honour-
ably in hope of being honoured ? . . .

If therefore you wish to inspire girls with a love of
virtue, without incessantly bidding them to be prudent,
give them a strong interest in being so; make them feel
the full value of prudence and you will make them love
it.   It is not enough to regard this interest as something
very remote; point it out to them now in the relations
of their own time of life and in the character of their
lovers.   Give them an idea of an honest man, of a man
of merit; teach them to recognize him and to love him
themselves; show them that such a man alone can make
them happy. . . .

i. Sophie at Fifteen.

Such is the spirit in which Sophie has been brought
up.   Her education has involved more care than difficulty, and has aimed rather at following her tastes than
at restraining them.   Let us now say a word concerning
her person; we may take it from the portrait which I
drew of her to Émile, or from his own idea of the wife
who can make him happy. . . .

Sophie is well-born and of a good disposition; she has
an exquisite sensibility, which makes it sometimes difficult
to check the activity of her imagination   Her mind is
less accurate than penetrating; her temper easy yet

uneven; her figure plain but agreeable; her countenance bespeaks a soul within and does not play you false; you may meet her with indifference, but you will not leave her without emotion. . . . She is fond of dress and understands it; her mother has no other chambermaid; she has good taste in setting herself off to advantage, but she has an aversion to costly attire; her dress always displays a combination of elegance and simplicity; she does not care for the striking but for the becoming. She does not know what colours are in fashion, but she knows to perfection what suits her own person. . . .

Sophie has natural abilities; she is sensible of them and has not neglected them: but, having had little opportunity of employing art in their cultivation, she has been satisfied to train an agreeable voice to sing accurately and with taste, and her little feet to move lightly, easily and gracefully, and to courtesy in any situation without constraint or awkwardness. Yet she has had no singing-master except her father and no dancing-mistress but her mother; an organist in the neighbourhood has given her some lessons in accompaniment on the harpsichord, which she has since improved by herself. . . .

But it is the various kinds of needlework which Sophie understands best and has been most carefully taught, even such neglected arts as cutting out and making her own dresses. There is no kind of needlework which she does not understand and perform with pleasure; but the employment which she prefers to all other is that of making lace, because there is none that requires a more agreeable attitude and none in which her fingers are employed with more grace and dexterity. She has likewise applied herself to all branches of housewifery. She understands the kitchen and the pantry, and knows the price and quality of provisions; she can keep accounts excellently and acts as housekeeper to her mother. No-one knows how to command properly without having first learned how to obey; this is the principle on which her mother thus employs her. [She prefers, however, not to get dirty.]

I mentioned that Sophie was greedy. This was her natural tendency; but she grew temperate from habit and remains so from principle. It is not the same with girls as with boys, whom you may safely govern up to a certain point by the appetite. This inclination is not without consequences in the case of women; it is too dangerous to indulge. . . .

Sophie's intellect is agreeable without being brilliant, thoughtful without being deep: it is the kind of intellect of which no-one speaks, because no-one realizes it to be greater or less than his own. It is enough to make her agreeable to those whom she is addressing, though it be not highly developed according to our usual ideas of women's education. For her mind has not been formed by reading, but only by the conversation of her parents, by her own reflexions, and by the observations which she has made in her own little world. Sophie is naturally cheerful; in her infancy she was a romping girl, but by degrees her mother took care to check her flighty airs. . . .

Sophie has too much sensibility to preserve a perfect equability of temper; but she has too kind a heart to let this sensibility be troublesome to others; she is the only sufferer. Say but a word to offend her, she will not pout, but her bosom will swell and she will wish to retire in order to give vent to her tears. In the midst of her weeping, let her father or mother call her back and say a single word, she instantly returns to laugh and play, expeditiously wiping her eyes and endeavouring to stifle her sobs.

Neither is she entirely free from caprice. Her temper, when pushed a trifle too far, degenerates into mutiny, and then she is apt to forget herself. But let her have time to reflect and her manner of repairing the offence will make it a merit. . . .

Sophie is not without religion, but her religion is simple and reasonable; it contains few dogmas and fewer devotional practices; or rather, being unacquainted with any essential practice but that of moral duty, she devotes her whole life to worshipping God by doing good. . . .

Sophie is but little acquainted with the world, yet she is obliging and attentive and does everything with a good grace. Her happy disposition is of more use to her than much art. She has a kind of politeness of her own, which does not show itself in set phrases or in slavishly following the changing vagaries of fashion, and does nothing from habit, but springs from a genuine desire to please, and succeeds in pleasing. . . .

So mature is her judgment and so entirely does she resemble a girl of twenty, though she is only fifteen, that she will not be treated as a child by her parents. . . . Should her character be such as I imagine, why should not her father speak to her somewhat as follows ?

" Sophie, you are now a big girl, and you will not always be a girl. We wish you to be happy, it is for our own sake that we wish it, because our happiness depends on yours. The happiness of a virtuous girl is to make an honest man happy; we must therefore think of marrying you and we must think of it in time, for your fate through life depends on your marriage and we cannot take too much time to reflect on it. . . . [Contrary to custom the choice of a husband is to be left to her. She must only marry one whom she loves, and should not aspire after a husband in too high a station : she should recognize her ignorance of the world and the deceptiveness of men, and she should consult her mother.]

[Sophie is based on a real original; so is the preceding address. But she based her ideal of a husband on Fénelon's *Télémaque* and, failing to find such a husband, pined away and died ! Not so, Sophie.]

2. PRACTICAL ADVICE: LETTER TO THE DUKE OF WURTEMBERG.

November 16, 1768.

Had I the misfortune to have been born a prince, to be a slave to the conventions of my station, to be compelled to maintain a court, a suite, a royal household, in other words a body of masters ; and had I in spite of my rank a spirit ardent enough to wish to be a man and to fulfil the lofty duties of a father, a husband and a citizen of the commonwealth of mankind—under such circumstances I should constantly experience a difficulty in reconciling such contradictory requirements, but in nothing more than in bringing up my children, in spite of the station which they hold as princes, for that in which they have been placed by Nature.

I should first say to myself, " You must not desire things which are incompatible ; you must not wish both to be and not to be. The difficulty which I wish to overcome is inherent in the circumstances of the case ; unless these can be changed, the difficulty remains. I must make up my mind that I shall not obtain all which I should like. Never mind, I will not be discouraged. Of the total which I desire, I will obtain the utmost possible; for that I can rely on my own zeal and character: but it is an attribute of the wise to bow to the yoke of necessity; when he has done what he can, he has done everything." Were I a prince, that is what I should say. Then I should go forward without hesitation and without fear; and, whatever my success, I should be satisfied. I think my satisfaction would be justified.

Your Highness must begin by convincing yourself clearly that no-one can fulfil a father's duties as well as the father himself, nor the mother's as well as the mother herself. I should like to fill twenty pages with the repetition of this one sentence; for I am convinced that everything depends on it.

Being a prince, you will rarely be able to act as a father; you will have too many other duties to perform. Your duties as a father must therefore necessarily be performed by others. Her Highness will be in nearly the same position.

These circumstances determine our first rule: take care that *some-one* loves your child. It is best that this some-one should be of her own sex. Her age is very difficult to decide. There are strong reasons why she should be young: but a young woman has too many other interests besides that of watching day and night over a child. This is an inevitable and decisive disadvantage. Do not therefore choose a young woman. A handsome woman would be still worse. If young you have to fear herself; if handsome, everyone who comes near her. It is better that she should be a widow than a spinster. If she has children, let none of them be near her, and see that they are all dependent on you. Do not have a woman of fine sentiments, much less an "intellectual" person. She needs just enough sense to understand your instructions without trying to improve on them. She *need* not be liberal, and she *must* not be lavish: rather, she should be of the careful type that looks to its own advantage. You cannot control a person of expensive habits; by her very failing you have a hold over a skin-flint. She must not be flighty or frivolous; for, apart from the inconvenience, it likewise indicates an unstable temperament, which is that of all foolish persons and is particularly to be avoided; for this reason, though lively people are more lovable, I always suspect them on account of their hastiness. As we shall not find a perfect woman, we must not expect everything; thus, gentleness is desirable, but, so long as she is gentle from conviction, she need not be so by temperament. I prefer a calm cool character to one that is gushing and capricious. In all points choose a safe in preference to a brilliant disposition. Brilliance is an actual disadvantage for the present purpose; a child who is destined to occupy a superior position may be spoiled by the merits of those who have brought her up. She expects all the world to be like them, and becomes unfair in her judgments towards her inferiors.

Further, do not look for intellectual culture; the mind acquires from study a superficial gloss and no more. If she is learned she will disguise her true self; you will understand her better if she is ignorant; should she be unable to read, so much the better, she will learn with her pupil. The only quality of mind which is indispensable is good sense.

I say nothing of her heart or her character, which must be taken for granted, since they are easily counterfeited. People are not so careful in concealing their other qualities; and from these a shrewd eye will detect those which are concealed. These questions may perhaps require more detailed consideration; but this is not the occasion.

I laid down as my chief rule that some-one must love the child. But how is this to be brought about? You cannot make her love the child by telling her to do so, especially before attachment has grown to be a habit. People sometimes derive amusement from the children of strangers, but they love only their own. She might love the child if she loved the parents; but people of your position have no friends, nor do people in any position find friends among their dependents. Consequently, since affection pre-supposes some motive, it can spring in this case from nothing except self-interest. Hence we reach a conclusion which is confirmed by many other circumstances that difficulties which cannot, in your station, be avoided must be obviated by payments. But do not think with others that money can do anything, that if you pay you are obeyed. It is untrue. I know nothing more difficult than for a rich man to use his wealth to gain his purposes. Money is a spring in the moral machine, but it always recoils on the hand which presses it.

We must consider a few points which are essential for our purpose.

We wish the governess to love the child: therefore the welfare of the governess must be bound up with that of the child. It is not enough that she is dependent on the services which she renders to the child; for people do not love those to whom they render service: furthermore, mercenary services are only apparent, real services may easily be neglected; and it is the latter which we need. She must, then, be dependent, not on her services, but on their success; her future must depend on the result of her training. Only on these terms will she

identify her own welfare with that of her pupil and
be driven to love her by the necessity of the case.
Then she will render substantial and not counterfeit
service, or rather, in serving her pupil, she will be
serving herself; all her work will be in her own
interest.

But who is to pass the verdict on her success? We
should be satisfied with the good faith of a fair-minded
father whose honour is well known: honesty is a sure
instrument in business, provided it be coupled with
penetration. But the father may die. The judgment
of women is not recognized as safe; and a mother's love
is blind. If the mother were constituted arbiter in
default of the father, the governess would either lose
confidence or become more intent on pleasing the mother
than on educating the child. I shall say no more on the
choice of the arbiter; it can only be decided on special
personal knowledge. The essential point is that the
governess should have complete confidence in the fairness of his judgment and should be convinced that she
will not lose the reward of her pains if she have succeeded and that, whatever she may plead, she will not
obtain them if she have failed. She must never forget
that payment is promised, not for her trouble, but for
its success.

I know well enough that, whether she have done her
duty or not, the price is bound to be paid. I am not
foolish enough (I know mankind too well) to imagine
that the arbiters, whoever they are, will proceed solemnly
to declare that a young princess from fifteen to twenty
years of age has been badly brought up. But, though
I realize this, the governess will not; or, if it occur to
her, will she not be sufficiently confident to risk her
happiness, her fortune and her livelihood on such a

chance. And we are not concerned here with the fairness of the award but with the training which is to win it.

Just as little strength attaches to pure reason, so pure self-interest has less than is commonly believed. Imagination is the only motive power. We must inspire the governess with imagination; by this faculty alone can we stir the passions. A promise of money payment is a potent force; but it is half lost in the distance of the prospect. If she calmly debits the delay against the payment, and the risk against the amount, her heart will be left cold. You must therefore so to speak expose the future to her gaze, to give it greater power; you must present it under forms which will bring it nearer, which will raise her hopes and will captivate her mind. But in this connexion I might easily lose my way if I attempted to exhaust all the possibilities, which vary according to time, place and people. Let me therefore take a single case which can be modified to suit any other combination of circumstances. I will assume that I am dealing with a quiet woman who loves ease and independence. I take this young lady for a country walk; she sees a little house, prettily situated, nicely arranged, with a court-yard, a garden, enough land to maintain the occupant, and enough charms to make her wish to live there. I see my governess enraptured; people always imagine themselves the owners of anything which will conduce to their happiness. At the height of her enthusiasm, I take her aside and say, "Bring up my daughter to my liking and you shall have all which you see." To prevent her from thinking this a mere casual remark, I draw up a legal agreement. There will not be a single unpleasant feeling in connexion with her work to which her imagination will not apply this house

as an antidote. Note, that this is only an illustration.
If the imagination is dulled by the distance of the
prospect, you can divide both period and payment into
several portions and even distribute them between several
persons; I see no difficulty or disadvantage in such a
course. "If in six years my child is so-and-so, you shall
have such and such a return." When this period is
completed, if the conditions are satisfied, the undertaking terminates and both sides are free.

Many other advantages will accrue from my proposed
expedient: but I cannot and need not mention them all.
The child will love her governess, especially if she begins
by being strict and if the child is not already spoiled.
The power of habit is natural and inevitable; it can fail
only through the fault of those who regulate it. Besides,
justice has its exact line and plummet, whereas com-
placency has no such rule, and consequently makes
children always exacting and discontented. We will
suppose the child to love her nurse and to know that her
fate depends on her success: let us deduce how she will
be led to act, as her intelligence and her affections
mature. Suppose that at a certain age the child is
wayward or rebellious. Imagine a serious and critical
situation when she refuses to listen to reason—such
occasions will be rare, as the reader can imagine. In
this difficult position the governess does not know what
to do; at last with a sad look she says to her pupil: "It
is all up, you are taking away the bread of my old
age." I do not imagine the daughter of such a father
to be a monster; the effect of this sentence is certain;
but it cannot be pronounced more than once. But we
may secure that the child repeats it constantly to herself; and this has many advantages. In any case, do
you think that a woman who can speak thus to her

pupil will not love her? We love those whom we have formed; it is natural. It is natural to love our own handiwork, especially when we look to it for our happiness. Our first requirement therefore is secured.

The second rule is that the governess should have her procedure thoroughly mapped out and should have complete confidence in its success. The memorandum of procedure which you should give her is very important. She must study it incessantly: she must know it by heart, better than an ambassador knows his instructions. What is still more important is that she should be perfectly convinced that there is no other way for her to attain your object and consequently her own.

It is not necessary for this purpose to give her the memorandum at once. You must first tell her what you wish done, and explain to her the mental and bodily ideal which you propose for her charge. On this point any objection or demur on her part is useless: you need give her no reasons for your wishes. But you must prove that your proposals are feasable and that they are feasable only by the means which you lay down. On this point you must reason with her fully. You must state your reasons clearly, simply, fully, and in language which she can understand. You must listen to her answers, her sentiments, and her objections; you must discuss them together at leisure, not so much on account of the objections themselves, which will probably be superficial, as in order to take this opportunity of probing into her mind and of convincing her that the means which you propose are the only means which are likely to succeed You must assure yourself that she is convinced on every point, not in words, but at heart. Not till then should you give her the memorandum, read it to her, consider it, expound it, perhaps amend it, and assure yourself that she understands it thoroughly.

In the course of the child's education unforeseen circumstances will frequently arise; the prescribed course will frequently not produce the expected results; the elements necessary to solve moral problems are very numerous, and a single omission falsifies the answer. There will therefore be frequent need of conferences, discussions, and explanations, which must never be refused, nay, must be made agreeable to the governess by the pleasure which you display in them. These moreover supply an excellent means of studying her character.

Details seem to me to be peculiarly the province of the mother. She ought to know the memorandum as well as the governess, but in a different manner. The governess will know it by rote; the mother, having received a more careful education and having a better trained mind, should be in a better position to generalize her ideas and to see it in all its bearings; further, as she takes a more living interest in it, she should be more concerned with the means for its accomplishment.

The third rule is that the governess should receive absolute authority over the child. Properly understood, this rule means no more than that every point should be regulated by the memorandum; for, if everyone regulates his conduct scrupulously by the memorandum, it must follow that everyone will always act in concert; except in some case of ignorance, against which it is easy to provide.

I have not lost sight of my object, though I have been compelled to take a very circuitous course. Many of the difficulties have already been removed; for our pupil will have little occasion to fear domestics when her fostermother has such an interest in watching over her. We will consider this point for a moment. There are in the household many general means of accomplishing everything, and without them we shall accomplish nothing. First, there must be good morals, the imposing image of virtue, before which all things bow, even vice itself; next, order and vigilance; and last and least important self-interest. I might add vanity, but the condition of servitude is too nearly allied to misery; vanity exercises its powerful influence only on those whose daily bread is secure.

In order that I may not repeat myself, your Highness will permit me to refer to the fourth part of the *Héloïse*, letter X. You will find there a summary of the maxims which appear to me to be fundamental whether the household be great or small for giving support to authority; but I admit the difficulties in the way of their accomplishment, because of all imaginable classes of mankind lackeys give us the fewest opportunities to influence their conduct. But all the reasonings in the world will not cause any institution to change its inherent character, will not compel the non-existent to exist, will not make lackeys other than lackeys.

The household of a prince can be enlarged or diminished without ceasing to be of a convenient size. I take this fact as the basis of my first maxim.

I. Reduce your household to the smallest dimensions possible; you will have fewer enemies and will be better served. If there is in your house a single unnecessary dependent, be sure that his presence does harm.

II. Be careful in the selection of those whom you retain, and give the preference to careful service over pleasant manners. Servants who assume pleasant airs before their master are always knaves. In particular, allow no dissipation.

III. Submit them in every matter to rules, even in their work, if what they do is to be of any value.

IV. Make it greatly to their interest to remain for a long time in your service; see that the longer they remain the more attached to it they grow, and that every day they stay they dread leaving more acutely. The reasons for this advice and the means for its accomplishment will be found in the reference quoted above.

Such are the conditions which I take for granted, since, though they involve considerable trouble, they ultimately depend on your own exertions. These being granted, I proceed.

Some time before speaking to them on the subject, you will occasionally direct the conversation at table to the education of your daughter, to the course which you intend to pursue, to the difficulties which you wish to overcome, and to your firm resolution to spare no pains which will ensure success. Probably your court will not have failed privately to criticize this extraordinary method of bringing up a child; they will have discovered it to be eccentric; you must justify it, but simply and in few words. Further, you must show your purpose much more on the moral than on the philosophical side. Her Highness, relying purely on her feelings, may intersperse some charming remarks. M. Tissot may add some reflexions which will be worthy of him.

People are so little accustomed to expect depth of feeling from the great, or to find them caring for virtue and interested in their children, that a short and well-managed conversation cannot fail to produce a great effect. But it is of the utmost importance that it should show no trace of affectation and should not be protracted too long. Attendants have penetrating eyes; the value would be lost if they suspect the conversation to be preconcerted; nor indeed should it be. A good father and a good mother may let their hearts speak in all simplicity; they will find suitable expressions on the spur of the moment; I can see the attendants behind the chairs prostrating themselves before their master from the bottom of their hearts. Such is the disposition which you must inspire and utilize in carrying out the regulations which you have to prescribe to them.

These regulations may be of two kinds, according to the opinion which you form of the state of your household and the morals of your attendants. If you believe that you can place a reasonable confidence in them founded on their own interests, it will need only a short, clear statement of the manner in which they must behave whenever they come near your child, in order that they may not counteract your scheme of education. But if, notwithstanding your precautions, you feel bound to mistrust what they might do or say in her presence, then the rule is still simpler, it reduces itself to a prohibition of going near her on any pretext whatever. Whichever of these two plans you adopt must be carried through without allowing any exceptions, and must be the same for all classes of your attendants, except those whom you specifically set apart for the service of your daughter, who cannot be too few in number or too carefully selected.

Some day, then, you assemble your attendants and in a simple and serious speech tell them that you conceive it to be the duty of a good father to exert the utmost care in bringing up the child whom God has given him. "Her mother and myself feel everything which injures our child. We wish to preserve her from harm; and, if God blesses our efforts, we shall not have to render Him account for faults and vices which she has contracted.

For this end we have to take precautions; I propose to explain those in which you are concerned; and I hope that in this matter you will show yourselves loyal servants, whose first duty is to aid in accomplishing that of your master."

Having laid down the rules which you prescribe for their observation, you add that those who are careful in following them can count on your kindness and even on your benefactions. "But I warn you at the same time," you add in louder tones, " that a single breach of duty, whatever be the delinquency, will be met by instant dismissal and loss of wages. These are the conditions on which I keep you; I have now given you all due warning, and those who do not wish to abide by them may go." Rules so little harassing will only make those leave who would have left without them: you will lose nothing by sending them away on the spot, and you will make a great impression. Perhaps at the beginning some stupid fellow will fall a victim, and he must do so. Even if he be the steward, if he is not sent away as a rogue, all is lost. But if they once see that you are in earnest and that they are under supervision, you will soon have little need to supervise them.

A number of minor consequential rules follow from these; but it is unnecessary to state them all, since this memoir is already too long. I will add but one important piece of advice, which will enable you to check any evil which you cannot anticipate; constantly examine your daughter with the greatest care and keep an attentive watch over her mental and bodily progress. If anything contrary to your rules is done in her presence, the impression is bound to be left on the child. Whenever you discover some new symptom, look carefully for the cause, and you will certainly find it. At a certain age there is always a remedy for evils which could not be prevented, provided that one can detect them and that one takes them in time.

These expedients are not all easy, and I will not answer absolutely for their success; nevertheless I believe that you can place a reasonable confidence in them, and I can see no alternative of which I can say the same. In a country so unexplored we must not look for beaten tracks; a novel and difficult enterprise cannot be executed by easy and common means.

Perhaps these are but the dreams of delirium. The comparison of what is and what should be has inspired me with the romantic spirit and has driven me far from reality. But when your Highness gives me orders, I obey. You have asked for my ideas; I have given them. I should be deceiving you if I gave you the wisdom of others in place of my own follies. In submitting them to the consideration of so shrewd a judge, I do not fear that they will have evil consequences.

IX

SUMMARY AND EXTRACTS FROM "ÉMILE," BOOK V., PART II.

[The *Émile* now assumes more of the form of a novel, which indeed it professed throughout, and recounts the love-making of the hero and heroine. At the close it contains, in an important digression, the first outline of the political theory which Rousseau afterwards elaborated in the *Social Contract*, and in connexion therewith a discussion of the educational value of travel.]

———————

1. [Reflexions on the choice of a wife. The choice should be based on affection : it is better for a man to marry below than above his rank, because he is in a position of authority ; but—]

IT is not desirable for a man of education to marry a woman that has had none, nor to marry into a rank where it cannot be found. But I had much rather have a plain girl, simply brought up and destitute of education, than a young woman of wit and learning, who would erect in my house a literary tribunal at which she would preside. A clever woman is a scourge to her husband, to her children, to her friends, to her servants, in short to everyone. From the lofty elevation of her genius, she despises all the duties of a woman,

and always begins to play the man after the example
of Mademoiselle de l'Enclos. Abroad, she is always
ridiculous and is very justly criticized, as is inevitable,
seeing that she has left her natural state and is unfitted
for that which she has assumed. Your great female
geniuses impose only on fools. No one is ignorant of
the artist or friend who holds the pen or pencil when
they work, or of the discreet man of letters who dictates
their oracles to them in private. All this deception is
unworthy of an honest woman. Even if she possessed
real abilities, it would only debase her to display them.
Her honour consists in being unknown, her glory in the
esteem of her husband, her pleasure in the happiness of
her family.

[Mediocrity is to be sought in everything, even in
beauty.]

2. [Émile and his tutor set out from Paris to find
Sophie. Advantage is taken of this journey to declaim
against the hurry of modern life and to extol the
happiness of leisurely travel, especially on foot, a method
which gives unique opportunities for observing scenery,
plants, rocks, etc.]

3. [They "lose their way" and are received at the
country-house of Sophie's father. In a digression
Rousseau exclaims :—]

Treatises on education give us long, useless, pedantic
discourses concerning the chimerical duties of children,
but not a word about the most difficult and most
important part of education, namely the critical transi-
tion from childhood to manhood. Could I render these
essays of any value, it would be chiefly in having enlarged on that essential part, omitted by all other
writers, without being discouraged from this under-

taking by a false delicacy or deterred by the difficulties of language. If I have written what ought to be done, I have written what I ought; I care not if I have written a romance. Human nature is a glorious romance! If it be found only in this work, is that my fault? It should be the every-day history of my fellow-beings; it is you who spoil it and turn it into a romance.

4. [They settle in the neighbourhood and Émile continues his love-making.]

5. [Émile is highly surprised when the tutor discovers that Sophie has some hesitation on the ground that she is not Émile's equal in wealth.]

Here then I am, the confidant of my two young people and the mediator of their courtship! A fine employment for a tutor! So fine that I never did anything in my life that raised me so high in my own esteem and afforded me such inward satisfaction.

[This difficulty removed, they become formally engaged.]

6. [Émile teaches Sophie music and everything he knows. A quarrel and how it was made up, the tutor always assisting.]

7. [How Émile has changed!] Thus do the scenes of life change! Each age has special springs which move it; but the man is always the same. At ten he is led by cakes, at twenty by a mistress, at thirty by amusements, at forty by ambition, at fifty by avarice. When does he make wisdom his sole pursuit?

If you wish to extend the effects of a good education throughout life, prolong the good habits of the child through youth; and when he has become all that he should be, see that he is the same at all times. This is the finishing stroke which you must give to your work. It is chiefly for this purpose that a youth ought to be still left under charge of a tutor; for there is little danger that he will not know how to make love by himself! Teachers, and especially parents, are wrong in supposing that the various modes of life are mutually exclusive, and that the man must renounce everything which he did as a boy. Were this the case, of what use would be our careful training of children, since the good or bad habits which they acquired would vanish with childhood, and when they entered on a different manner of life, they would necessarily assume different ways of thinking?

The continuity of memory is broken only by violent injuries, that of character only by violent passions. Although our tastes and inclinations change, this change, even if it be sometimes abrupt, is moderated by habit. In the succession of tastes, as in a good sequence of colour, the able artist should render the transitions imperceptible, should blend and mingle the tints, and, in order that none should be too glaring, should diffuse several over the whole work. This rule is confirmed by experience. People of immoderate passions change their affections, tastes and sentiments every day, and are constant in nothing but their inconstancy; but a man of regular life constantly returns to his ancient habits, and even in his old age, does not lose his relish for the pleasures which he loved in his infancy.

If you can secure that, in advancing to a new stage, your pupil does not despise that which he has quitted, and that, in contracting new habits, he still preserves the old, that he always wishes to do what is right without regard to the time when the habit was formed—then, and then only, have you made your work secure. You may then be sure of your pupil to the end of his days; for the most dangerous crisis is the moment which you are now watching. As it is a period to which we always look back with regret, it is difficult at a later stage to lose the tastes which have been preserved to its close; whereas, if any are now discontinued, we never afterwards recover them.

[The rest of the section consequently describes his old habits—*e.g.*, the pursuit of a trade, kindness to neighbour, and constant activity, continued simultaneously with his love-making.]

8. [Long address by the tutor, ending in a proposal that, as a married man must be a citizen, Émile, before marrying, must learn the nature of civil institutions by means of travel, which will enable him to compare those of different countries.]

9. It is a question which has frequently been debated whether it is good for young people to travel. Were the question put in another form, whether it is a good thing that men have travelled, perhaps there would be less room for dispute. Misuse of books kills knowledge. Believing that we know what we have read, we think ourselves excused from learning it. Too much reading only makes presumptuous ignoramuses. In no age of literature has there been so much reading as in the present, and in no age has there been less learning: no country in Europe has produced so many histories and stories of travel as France, and none is less acquainted with the genius and manners of other nations. Such a multitude of books makes us forget the book of the world; or, if we still peruse it, every man sticks to his own leaf. . . . A Parisian imagines he knows men, and

he knows only Frenchmen : in a city that is always full of foreigners, he looks upon every stranger as an extraordinary phenomenon without a parallel in the universe. . . .

Let us leave the boasted assistance of books to those who are credulous enough to be content with them. . . . I hold it as an incontestable maxim that a person who has only seen one people, instead of knowing men, knows only the people with whom he has lived. Here, then, is another method of stating the question about travel, " Is it enough for a well-educated person to be acquainted only with his fellow-countrymen, or is it also requisite that he should know mankind in general ?" This admits of no dispute or doubt. And thus you perceive how the solution of a difficulty sometimes depends on the manner of stating it.

But, in order to study mankind, must we travel over the whole globe ? Must we visit Japan in order to observe Europeans ? To know the species, must we know all the individuals ? No; there are people who so closely resemble one another that it is not worth while to study them separately. If you have seen ten Frenchmen, you have seen all, and, though this remark cannot be applied to the English and some other nations, yet it is certain that every nation has its own specific character, which can be inferred from the observation, not indeed of a single member, but of several. The observer who has compared ten different nations knows men, as he who has seen ten Frenchmen knows the French.

In order to learn, it is not enough to traverse a country ; you must travel in the right way. To observe, you must have eyes, and you must turn them towards the object which you wish to examine. There are many people who learn even less from travelling than from books, because they are ignorant of the art of thinking : in reading they are at least guided by the author, but in travelling they can see nothing for themselves. . . .

As the least polished nations are generally the wisest, those who travel least travel to best advantage ; because, being less advanced in frivolous researches and less occupied with the objects of our idle curiosity, they give their whole attention to matters of real utility. I know none but the Spaniards who travel in this manner : while a Frenchman runs after the artists, while an Englishman is planning something antique, and a German is visiting the learned with his album, the Spaniard silently notices the government, the manners and the order of a country ; and of the four he is the only one who on his return brings back any observations which will be of use to his country.

The ancients travelled little, read little, and wrote little ; yet we see by their extant works that they observed one another better than do our contemporaries. . . .

There is a great difference between travelling in order to see countries and in order to see peoples. The former is always the object of the curious, and the latter only an accessory. This order must be reversed by one who wishes to reflect. A child observes things, because he is not yet able to observe men. Men ought to begin by observing their fellows ; and afterwards may notice things, if they have time.

It is therefore bad reasoning, because travel is generally badly conducted, to conclude that it is useless. But granting its utility, does it follow that it is suitable for everyone ? Far from it ; it is adapted to very few, to such only as are strong-minded enough to listen to error without being misled, and to look on vicious examples without being corrupted. Travelling encourages a man's natural bent, and completes his character, whether good or bad. On his return from his foreign tour, a man is what he will be all his life : more men return from their travels vicious than virtuous, because more are inclined to vice than to virtue when they go out. Badly educated and badly conducted young people contract during their travels all the vices of the races with whom they mix, and none of the virtues which are associated with them. Those who are virtuously inclined, whose good disposition has been rightly trained, and who go abroad with a real intention to learn, will return better and wiser than they set out. . . .

All actions which are guided by reason must submit to rules. Foreign travel, considered as a part of education, must be regulated by its own rules. To travel for travel's sake is to be a tramp : to travel for instruction is too vague an object, since instruction, without a definite end, means nothing. [He now comes to what the aim is.] After a youth has considered his physical relations to other objects and his moral relations to other men, it remains for him to consider his civil relations to his fellow-citizens. For this purpose he must begin by studying the nature of government in general and its different forms, and must end by considering the particular government under which he was born, in order to determine whether it be right for him to live under it. Every man, on coming of age and becoming his own master, has a right, which nothing can abrogate, to renounce the contract that binds him to the community, by quitting the country in which it is established.

[The tutor makes a long address, ending thus :—] " Should we succeed [in finding an ideal government] you will have found the true happiness for which so many have searched, and you will have no cause to complain that you have wasted your time. If we fail, you will be cured of a delusion; you will make the best of an inevitable evil and submit to the law of necessity."

I question whether all my readers will perceive the drift of the investigation which is thus set before him. I am convinced that, if, on his return from his travels, begun and continued with this aim, Émile be not perfectly acquainted with all matters relating to government, to national customs, and to state affairs of every kind, either he must be totally wanting in capacity or I in judgment.

10. [Section on political theory, afterwards elaborated in the *Social Contract*.]

11. [He returns to the subject of travel.] I have mentioned a cause which generally defeats the utility of travel. What renders it still less useful to young people is the manner in which their travels are usually conducted. Their tutors, more desirous to amuse than to instruct, carry them from town to town, from palace to palace, from circle to circle; or, if they are men of learning and culture, they make them spend their time in going through libraries, visiting antiquarians, turning over old records, and copying ancient inscriptions. In each country they busy themselves with past ages. They might as well be occupied with other countries. having traversed Europe at great expense, given up alternately to frivolity and to boredom, they return without having observed any interesting object and without having learned any fact which is conducive to their real advantage.

All capitals are alike. You find in them a mixture of

all nations and all customs : it is not there that you must go to study peoples. . . . It is to the distant provinces where there is less trade and communication, where fewer strangers travel, and where the inhabitants are more fixed and more seldom change their rank or fortune, that you must go to learn the genius and manners of a nation. Look at the capital on your way, but make your real observations in the remote parts of the country. . . .

12. After having employed nearly two years in travelling through several of the great and many of the smaller states of Europe, after having learned two or three of the principal languages and noticed what was really remarkable whether in the natural history, in the arts, or in the inhabitants, Émile, labouring under impatience, reminded me that our time was almost expired. [He has found that all ties of ownership restrict the liberty of the owner, but he will retain his property, knowing that he can always earn his living by his trade if it is taken away.]

[The return and marriage.]

SUBJECT INDEX

I. BRANCHES OF EDUCATION

TRAINING OF THE SENSES.

CONDITION of infant as regards sense-perception, 78-79 ; acquisition of idea of extension, 81-82 ; general principle of learning observation through activity, 121-124 ; training of sight and touch, and their co-ordination, 126-132 ; hearing, 137.

PHYSICAL DEVELOPMENT.

General principles of health, 76-77 ; directions against excessive precaution, 36-37, 63-64, 88 ; food, 139 ; clothing, 124 ; sleep, 125 ; bathing, 77, 124 ; exercise, 36, 93, 126, 130-132, 137-139 ; medicine, 76 ; physical training precedes mental, 28, 99, 108.

BODILY SKILL.

Running, 130-132 ; swimming, 126 ; games, 137-139 ; gymnastics and athletics, 66-68 ; gardening and agriculture, 101-103, 169 ; handicraft, 163, 167-172 ; needlework, 221-223 ; girls' accomplishments, 225-227 ; dependence of intellectual on bodily training, 121-124, 126-137.

INTELLECTUAL TRAINING.

Differentiation according to innate ability and temperament, 29-34 ; postponement of study, 26-28, 48-49, 98-99, 108-110.

SUBJECTS : Reading, 50-51, 119-120, 223 ; writing, 121 ; arithmetic, 223 ; geometry, 109, 135-137 ; drawing, 132-135 ; speech, 86, 227 ; singing, 137, 225-226 ; fables, 50, 115-119, 198 ; literature, 196, 211-216 ; history 113-114, 189-196 ; geography, 112, 148-153, 160-161 ; natural science, 124, 153-158, 174-175 ; languages, 111, 214, 262 ; classics, 112, 193-195, 211-216 ; economics, 163-167 : politics, 189, 257-262 ; limits of women's intellectual training, 232.

MORAL TRAINING.

Non-moral condition of infants, 84, 97-98 ; liberty, but no domination, 34-42, 46-47, 53-54, 83-86 ; dependence, not on men but on things, 91-97 ; no direct moral instruction in childhood, 95-96, 99-103, 105, 115-119 ; example, 105-107 ; first introduction of quasi-moral ideas, 163-170 ; summary of results

263

up to fifteen, 177-178 ; training of the emotions and sentiments after adolescence, 179-188 ; giving of social ideas, 179-196 ; lessons of experience, 196-200 ; religion, 200-204 ; instruction concerning sex, 204-208 ; moral training of girls, 223-225, 227-235.

PARTICULAR VIRTUES AND VICES : Equanimity, 40-43, 47, 82-86 ; courage, 87-88, 128-129, 138, 177 ; self-reliance, 92-94, 157 ; moderation of desires, 89-91, 189 ; gluttony, 139, 237 ; sexual virtue, 204-208, 254-255 ; gambling and extravagance, 197 ; luxury, 167, 184 ; idleness, 168, 223 ; truthfulness 104-105 ; vanity, 44-45, 155-156, 183, 197 ; benevolence and altruistic virtues, 181-188, 199 ; envy, 97, 126, 182 ; recognition of property, 100-103 ; kindness to animals, 199.

II. SCIENCES UNDERLYING EDUCATIONAL VIEWS

PSYCHOLOGY.

Heredity as factor in human differences in contrast to environment, 30-33 ; non-social character of children, 94, 159.

Sensational level, 78-80 ; development of perception, 80-82 ; further training of perception, 126-132 ; memory, 48-49, 109, 158-159 ; imagery, 109 ; late development of reason, 28, 95, 109-110 ; conception and reasoning, 172-175 ; imagination, 90-91, 135-136 ; relation of language to thought, 111.

Rudimentary affective consciousness, 80-82 ; development of sentiments and emotions, 179-188 ; fear, 81, 128, 177 ; instinct of self-preservation, 179-181 ; sense of justice, 83 ; curiosity, 147-148.

Active tendency, 36, 93 ; constructive instinct, 84, 101 ; imitation, 106-107 ; habit, 57-58, 80, 199, 255-256.

LOGIC.

Analysis and synthesis, 152 ; deduction, 135-136 ; induction, 157, 174-175 ; historical evidence, 192 ; systems of knowledge, 154-155.

ETHICS.

Moral faculty Reason, 84, 98 ; moral criterion negative, 107 ; ethics dependent on politics, 189 ; obligations based on Society, 168 ; moral sanction of religion, 204 ; inherent goodness of man, 29, 55, 84, 97-98, 190 ; development of virtue in individual, 179-186.

SOCIAL SCIENCES.

State of Nature contrasted with Society, 59-60, 189 ; Robinson Crusoe as type of natural man, 162 ; Society based on mutual wants, 183-184 ; wants partly economic, 163 ; consequent duty of work, 168 ; order of the industries, 164-165, 168-169 ; money, 166-167 ; evils due to Society, 55, 190 ; evils based on number of artificial wants, 89-95, 189 ; consequent condemnation of luxury, 167, 216.

Place of women in Society, 217-219 ; parentage and family life State duties, 72-75 ; claims of patriotism, 59-61, 65, 69-70.

Inequality of capacity, 31-34 ; poor do not need education, 33-34, 71 ; education needed for the State, 34 ; State education, 60-61, 64-70 ; individual education, 61-63.

III. EDUCATIONAL AGENTS AND INSTRUMENTS

AGENTS.

The State, 60-61, 64-70.
The family, 52-54, 72-75.
The father, 46, 54, 74-75, 239-252.
The mother, 72-74, 218, 220-221, 224, 234.
The tutor, 24-25, 107-108, 134, 140, 188, 197-198, 206-208, 255-256.
The governess (for girls), 240-247.
Servants, 38, 248-251.

INSTRUMENTS.

STIMULI : Imitation, 126 ; consciousness of improvement, 135 ; necessity, 97, 159 ; curiosity, 147-148, 150-151, 152, 154 ; constructiveness, 157-158 ; prizes in games only, 67-68, 130-132 ; present interest, 49-51, 119-121 ; wrong kinds, 97, 110, 126, 159.

RESTRAINTS : Necessity, 35, 92, 97 ; natural consequences, 47, 92, 103-105, 108 ; tutor's arrangement of environment, 107-108 ; control in the family, 39-47.

See also in General Index under Commands abolished, Compulsion to learn abolished, Control.

GENERAL INDEX

Women : characteristics and duties, 217-219, 230 ; principles of education, 219-221 ; sensibility and reason, 229-231 ; fickle, 224 ; tact, 231 ; condemnation of clever, 253-254

Words, teaching of, 110

Work not distinguished from play by child, 143 ; distinction begun, 159 ; a social duty, 168. *See also* Manual work

Writing, 121

Wurtemberg, Duke of, letter to 239-252

Xenophon, 193